THE
MONDAY
MINDSET

THE MONDAY MINDSET

Positive Mindset = Positive Outcome

Joshua Brae Bugg

XULON PRESS

Xulon Press
2301 Lucien Way #415
Maitland, FL 32751
407.339.4217
www.xulonpress.com

Unless otherwise indicated, Scripture quotations taken from the Holy Bible, New Living Translation (NLT). Copyright ©1996, 2004, 2007 by Tyndale House Foundation. Used by permission of Tyndale House Publishers, Inc.

Printed in the United States of America.

ISBN-13: 978-1-6322-1931-2
Ebook: 978-1-6322-1932-9

Table of Contents

HOW TO USE THIS BOOK

There are fifty-two weeks in a calendar year; that is fifty-two Monday mornings. I believe this book will help you become a better version of who you were created to be. I hope it builds your faith, inspires you to have courage, and uplifts your thoughts throughout this year as you read each lesson. Each lesson is written in the form of weeks (ex. Week 24.) Before you continue, please receive this word in your spirit: You are a child of God, He is aware of everything, and He loves you eternally. You do not need to be perfect for Him to use your gifts and empower you to create greatness in your reality. Renew your mind each week, be yourself, serve the needs of others, and let your light shine!

ISAIAH 40:31

"But those who hope in the Lord will renew their strength. They will soar on wings like eagles; they will run and not grow weary, they will walk and not be faint."

MINDSET: Each lesson will conclude with a mindset renewal key at the bottom in bold letters.

Introduction
A WINNING MINDSET LEADS THE WAY

"If you take responsibility for yourself
you will develop a hunger to accomplish
your dreams."

Les Brown

You will not reach any worthwhile dream if you allow your own mentality to trip you up. The human brain weighs approximately three pounds, but it has billions of microscopic cells. These cells are called neurons and they are designed to transfer information.

THE TRANSFER

What valuable information are you not transferring into your reality? Your mindset going into each week can be likened to that of a runner's baton used in relay races. Each team of runners must believe that they will cross the finish line of success that eludes so many. It takes an immense amount of practice and discipline to learn how to properly transfer the baton in a relay race. One mishandled transfer can ruin the desired outcome of the race for the entire team. One negative thought can throw you off track for the rest of the week. Your mind is like a baton, it must be handled with intention, purpose, and precision. Whether you are an athlete, student, educator, doctor, business owner, or anything else not mentioned in this short list – you've got to develop a hunger that allows you to stride decisively in the direction of your dreams. Keep your eyes on the prize!

YOU MUST BELIEVE

Before you continue reading any further, you have got to understand that a detour can never capture more of your mental focus than your dreams. If something is worthwhile, it is worth your time and undivided attention. As you begin to envision your finish line, remember this: you will not win if your mindset begins in a place of doubt. To believe simply means to have confidence that something will happen, no matter what!

Mindset: As you enter the exchange zone, with your baton in hand, you must maintain confidence if you are going to successfully transfer from this level to the next!

NOT GOING BACK TO NORMAL

"Routines are normal, natural, healthy things. Most of us take a shower and brush our teeth every day. That is a good routine. Spiritual disciplines are routines. That is a good thing. But once routines become routine you need to change your routine."

Dr. Mark Batterson

There comes a time in each of our lives when we must recognize that we can improve. In the words of former Austin Peay standout basketball player Fernandez Lockett, *"Let's get better!"*

IMPROVEMENT

What routines have become normal in your life that need to be critiqued and changed? To truly change, you must be willing to confront your character. You used to wake up early, open that door, send that encouraging text message, pay for the coffee for that car behind you, treat others the way you want to be treated, etc. Now, you have become stale and uninspired, unthankful for the things you used to pray for. Normal has become woven into your mentality and you have become exhausted with chasing greatness. Isaiah 40:30 NLT says: "Even youths will become weak and tired, and young men will fall in exhaustion."

DOCUMENTATION

A great opportunity in life as believers is the ability to document, document, document. Documentation can be described as evidence you can use to serve as a record. Write down where you started and where you want to go. Keep a journal, ask God to reveal His will for your life, and believe that He has designed your race to reach great heights. God does not promise to give us everything we ask for, but I am confident He wants us to enjoy the journey. When we document, it provides us with an in-hand reminder that we have come a long way. Take time today to write down the hills and valleys of your life. Understand that change is inevitable and that He provides grace during your exhaustion.

QUIT FEELING INADEQUATE

Christ is within you; therefore, you are enough! The Apostle Paul wrote about the strength of weakness in 2 Corinthians. In a letter to a church he founded on his initial visit to Corinth, Paul reminds us that God wants to comfort us all. He went through many hardships and still managed to show us how to live generously. Whatever your greatest weakness is, understand that you are not normal and that is okay. 2 Corinthians 12:8-9 says: "Three different times I begged the Lord to take it away. Each time he said, 'My grace is all you need, My power works best in weakness.'" God wastes nothing! God uses our routines to teach us there is a better way. If God allows something to remain in our lives, it must have a purpose – even if we cannot understand it. He uses our mistakes, our doubts, and our regrets to build our endurance. We must run after our destiny. Do not stroll, do not mosey along – we must run!

Mindset: You have officially moved into the starting position of self-improvement. You will run this race and not grow weary, because God created you to be abnormal. You are not normal and that is okay!

DEAD OR PLANTED?

"Big ideas come from forward-thinking people who challenge the norm, think outside the box, and invent the world they see inside rather than submitting to the limitations of current dilemmas."

T.D. Jakes

You should never make a permanent decision because of a temporary circumstance. The amazing thing about the Bible is that we do not simply read it; it reads us.

VISION

Do you feel like you are unworthy to lead at a high level? Your life is not measured in the amount of seeds you have in your possession, but in the amount of seeds you willingly release into the soil of the unknown. Unworthiness is a lie from Satan. Under no circumstance should you remain within the prison of your current dilemma. A dilemma is simply a situation in which you must make a difficult choice – usually between two negative outcomes. Your destiny is greater than your dilemma. Proverbs 16:3 says: "Commit your work to the Lord, and your plans will be established."

FIRM FOUNDATION

When something dies, it is gone forever – except when it goes through the resurrection process. The beautiful thing about the Christian faith is that Jesus gave us the ability to conquer our doubts with forward thinking. Take a moment to consider the work that lies ahead of you this week. The people you will encounter, the responsibilities that await. Now, commit your work to honoring God and execute your plan to the best of your abilities. You were created to lead at a high level. You have the power to create and maintain positive relationships in your life. Each day matters to God, so each day should matter to you. By serving the needs of others above your own, you become the greatest type of leader. Your platform of influence is every place where you step foot this week. Be ready to use your time, talent, and treasure to make deposits into the soil of uncertainty.

YOU NEVER KNOW

What is a seed? According to the Bible, seed is the Word of God. A seed can go into a variety of soils for various amounts of time and produce something new. Seeds are coated with a protective layer, and it takes time for that layer to dissolve and the embryo within to produce what it is intended to produce. Whether something is viewed as dead or planted in your life matters. Your heart is a type of soil that can produce great things.

Your mentality is either talking you into scattering seed or holding onto it – in fear of becoming stuck within the soil of doubt. As Jesus taught from the boat in Matthew 13, He gave a clear picture of how to scatter our seed. Matthew 13:9 says: "Anyone with ears to hear should listen and understand." Think beyond what you see. Allow your mind to envision outside of the box. You have seeds within you, and it is time for you to let them go – you must sow!

Mindset: God will not allow you to stay in your comfort zone. God knows how to scatter you. You are His seed. If your vision is big enough, He will put you in a place where you must trust Him. It is not dead, it is planted!

NOT FOR SALE

"God is looking for people who are willing to exercise their minds to be transformed and renewed."

Michael Slaughter, Momentum for Life

When the flood recedes in your mind, you will recognize that mediocrity is not for you and your mind is not for sale. The moment you glimpse the future God has for planned for you, nothing will prevent you from reaching it – if you will believe it first in your mind.

COST OF ADMISSION

Determination will keep us focused on our dreams when the waters of life keep us up at night. While comparison will allow someone that has given their heart to Jesus to secretly doubt in their minds.. When a rainy day occurs in life, it is critical to stay focused on God's word. It is not about wanting success; it is about how we go about achieving it. Human beings can have the right desires and go about obtaining them the wrong way.

No matter how big and tough we think we are, life will knock us down and there will be rainy days! The only way to remain determined during the storms of life is to allow God's word to transform our thinking and sustain a positive mindset within us during the entire process.

THE WAY YOU THINK

The things we allow to get planted in our minds will produce a harvest of some sorts. The Lord was pleased with Noah and the way his life demonstrated obedience in the flood. Genesis 8:22 says: "As long as the earth remains, there will be planting and harvesting, cold and heat, summer and winter, day and night." Noah did not sell out and disobey what God commanded him to do; instead, he remained within the ark as God told him.

Mindset: You are in the right position, but your mind must change. Today, as you enter a new week, make sure that you get ready for pressure. When pressure gets applied, what is in you will come out. Your mind is not for sale, and you are being called to excellence!

WEEK 4

REJECTION LEADS TO DIRECTION

"If you don't fail, you're not even trying."

Denzel Washington

Three. Two. One. Time is out. You got the shot off, over the much taller and more athletic defender, but you missed. Failure. You lost, right? Sometimes we worry about the wrong stuff. Sometimes we feel rejected from success because we missed the mark and fell short. It is in these moments that we can gain our greatest sense of direction, if we learn to view them as opportunities.

TURN LEFT

Do you know who you are? You must understand who you are. When you feel like you are not going the right way, turn left. It may not look like you are any-where close to making that shot, getting that job, mar-rying that person, buying that house, paying off that debt, etc. However, there is good news: at least you are trying. Plus, if you are willing to try – God will do the

9

rest. God is getting ready to give you victory, but you must build it!

BUILD THE BEAST, SIMON

If you ask God to open the door and use your talents, He will hear you. Once you have shown God the bold humility and courage to ask Him – sit back and keep building the beast. Take that thing that you failed at and build on it. Who you say God is and who you say you are determines your direction in life, so, you must learn to monitor your inner dialogue. Matthew 16:17-18 says: "Jesus came back, 'God bless you, Simon, son of Jonah! You did not get that answer out of books or from teachers. My Father in heaven, God himself, let you in on this secret of who I really am. And now I'm going to tell you who you are, really are. You are Peter, a rock. This is the rock on which I will put together my church, a church so expansive with energy that not even the gates of hell will be able to keep it out.'"

Mindset: With God, you will never lose. Build the beast!

WEEK 5

THE LAMP THAT LEADS

"Your eye is like a lamp that provides light
for your body. When your eye is healthy,
your whole body is filled with light."

Jesus, Matthew 6:22

Where your focus goes, your energy will follow. It is difficult but possible to remain focused on what is positive during a negative moment. If you train your eyes to see the good, it will be a gamechanger in your life.

POSTIVE ENERGY

How do you encourage and motivate yourself? Music. Exercise. Reading Scripture. Everyone gets to choose what kind of year we are going to have. We all get to pick how we will energize our day to day lives. Spread your wings like an eagle and soar into your bright future.

PLUGGED IN

Your body is the very thing that will take you to the places you want to go. Your health matters. The things you choose to consume matter. Make wise decisions and filter the things you put into your body. This is not simply a discussion on food or drink. It is an analysis of what you listen to, what you choose to read, the people you surround yourself with, the decisions you make with your money, etc. You are plugged into something or someone. Make sure it is filling your body with the type of light that satisfies your soul.

QUICK STOP

Pause right now and praise God for another day, for the breath in your body, for where you are, and for the week that lies ahead. Remember that you can accomplish great things if you stay connected to the right energy sources. When you learn to keep your eyes focused on what is positive in life, a light will radiate from within you!

Mindset: Let your eyes lead you like a lamp in the dark!

SERVANT LEADERSHIP

> "Servant leadership is all about making the goals clear and then rolling your sleeves up and doing whatever it takes to help people win. In that situation, they don't work for you; you work for them."
>
> *Ken Blanchard*

The greatest leader within your circle of influence is always the one who serves.

JESUS

Have you thought about your ability to process the concept of humility and apply it to your life? In any situation, trust requires consistency. When talking about leadership, you must consider what a good leader looks like in the flesh. As you begin to analyze the character of Jesus in the Bible, it becomes clear that He is a different type of leader. The religious leaders of that time came under criticism from Jesus. He called out the fact that they did not do as they said. Matthew 23:5

says: "Everything they do is for show." He continued to say this in verse 11: "The greatest among you must be your servant."

THE THREE SERVANTS

We all have started at the bottom of the professional mountain, attempting to work our way up. Each of us have ambitious dreams that were given to us before we were born. While teaching on the Kingdom of Heaven, Jesus used the illustration of a man who went away on a long trip. Before he went away on that trip, he entrusted three servants with different amounts of money. Think of this money as the talents we possess, resources we have, opportunities in front of us, time on our jobs, etc. Now we need to ask ourselves: Are we making the most of what we have been given? The parable recorded in Matthew goes on to paint a picture of how God is displeased when we waste our time and bury our talents. Fear is a common reason why people do not serve the world to their highest abilities. As we see in verse 24-25: "Then the servant with one bag of silver came and said, 'Master, I knew you were a harsh man, harvesting crops you did not plant and gathering crops you did not cultivate. I was afraid I would lose your money, so I hid it in the earth. Look, here is your money back.'"

THE WORK DON'T LIE

You have been placed in a specific location for a purpose. That purpose may be to encourage others. That purpose may be to take care of someone materially. That purpose may be to share the good news of Christ with the community. Regardless of what you think, there is a greater purpose – even in suffering. Be excited while you work. Double everything God gives you. Believe that the needs of others are more important than your own. Work as hard as you can to cultivate the world around you. You have been tasked with making this world a better place. Les Brown: "Everything you do and every decision you make should be from a place of good. You should always be striving to make the world a better place." When your time is up, make sure that you have worked hard, loved others, and lived self-lessly. Real leaders work just as hard as the people they are leading!

Mindset: Be faithful with a little and watch it multiply!

CREATE THE STANDARD

"Don't tempt me with a good time."

Dr. Trae Weiss

Right now, in this very moment, you are creating something. The way you envision your life determines your actions. Your actions create a standard as time goes by. Block the noise, aim high, and chase after the elusiveness of greatness. You were born to be great and your loved ones are watching you every step of the way.

HANDS ON

What life experiences have you been given that can help catapult you into your destiny? Your dreams will not happen without a fight. You must not blame anyone else for your own inconsistent behavior. Challenge yourself to be more consistent, more dedicated, and more creative. The best way to learn and improve your mindset is through hands-on experience. Regardless of your line of work, you are leaving an example for others to see. It is easy for someone to say how dedicated they will be once they get the promotion. Not you, you are going to be dedicated right now, and that is exactly how you will get the promotion. Get ready for your fight!

EVERYTHING YOU GOT

God is waiting on you. Do you have the courage to think beyond your current set of circumstances? Do you believe you have within you the ability to excel despite the adversity? Is your mind being challenged to grow and expand through the dirty places of life? Your thoughts are seeds for your creativity. Your decisions are seeds. Your workplace is the foundation for your thoughts to be sown as seeds. Are you sowing? Are you afraid to live your best life? Are you making the most of your time? Give life everything and it will give back to you; pressed down, shaken together, and running over.

Mindset: The seeds in your hands + maximizing your time = creating a high standard for the next generation.

WEEK 8

CALLED TO THE AIR

"You cannot be anything you want to be
– but you can be a lot more of who you
already are."

Don Clifton

You are strong enough to fly over the everyday problems that slow you down, but you must be willing to jump into the takeoff phase like the Wright brothers.

THE DETOUR OF DOUBT

It is more important that you be happy in your own home than anywhere else you can possibly go. Your home, the place you lay your head at night, is the place that must be able to recharge your peace. Before you take off flying toward your destiny and your greatest dreams, consider this: Do you have a healthy place to lay your head? As a baby, Moses was hidden in the Nile River. Why? Because Pharaoh was determined to kill every male newborn in Egypt. As he grew up and time passed, he came into a moment of destiny with God. A moment where God was calling him to do something he thought he was not capable of doing. So what, you did not get the promotion? So what, you struggle to pay the bills? So what, your childhood was turbulent at times? Each detour you face will deter you from reaching your highest altitude. God knows if you understood the entire picture of where He is taking you, you would turn back too early. Listen and understand. You cannot live out your dreams if you allow doubt to live in your mind. Your Red Sea moment will be here before you know it, but will you be ready for takeoff? Exodus 13:17 says: "God said, 'If the people are faced with a battle, they might change their minds and return to Egypt.'" You are no longer allowed to turn back and live from within your comfort zone.

OUTSIDE

Now that your mind is in order, God is calling you to stretch outside of your comfort zone. If you learn to look forward to the turbulent challenges of flying in the air, you will soar to unimaginable heights. Your mindset is like the wings of an eagle, but you will not elevate to the next level if you remain doubtful. Wake up, stretch your legs, prepare for the day, and get outside. As you open the door, remain confident that He is always leading you. God will sustain you, and He will never forsake you.

BE MORE OF YOU

Doubt can come from unfairly comparing yourself to others. So, do not compare your life to theirs. The opposite of doubt is certainty. One thing is for certain:

you are perfectly you. You are stronger than your past, and you are more than a conqueror. Romans 8:37 says: "No, despite all these things, overwhelming victory is ours through Christ, who loved us." It is time to get back in the fight and soar to great heights. Focus on the goal and be confident that your wings are ready for flight.

Mindset: God always uses turbulence to develop our strength. It is time to use turbulence to your advantage; think positive thoughts, spread your wings, and fly high.

WEEK 9

RENEWED STRENGTH

"Only those who risk going too far, can
possibly find out how far one can go."

Dr. Eric Thomas

Find a way to make it. You might have been thrown
in the woods, but you will find your way out. You
are the walking example of what endurance looks like.

THE WORKOUT

How far are you willing to go once the winds of
leadership begin to hit you hard? To find out how strong
you are, you must be willing to exhaust all your mental
fortitude in a specific direction. You submit to a vision,
a goal, a task, and a purpose. A workout is supposed to
be challenging. In many ways, your life is a gymnasium
for you to work out. Sports have the unique ability to
teach us invaluable life lessons that we do not receive
anywhere else. For many of us, the road to success is
beset with a multitude of failures. You must have a clear

vision for your life; one that is energized by your core values and practical ways to capitalize on your strengths.

DISCOVER YOUR STRENGTHS

There are times in team sports when everything is going great, and times when nothing goes right. Some like to think that this is a cue signaling that you and the team are about to fail or lose. Renewed strength is developed through the sudden changes in battles. Battles in sports, battles against doubt, battles with addictions, battles in your relationships, etc. In those moments of sudden change, take the risk of going too far. Tell yourself, even though something negative just occurred, or something did not go as planned: you are still in the game. As time remains in your life, embrace failure, and use it to propel your life forward as a stronger version of yourself. Even though this or that happened, I will become more determined to reach my dreams and goals. The book of James talks about putting our Christian faith into action. Faith and endurance go hand in hand. James 1:2-4 says: "Dear brothers and sisters, when troubles of any kind come your way, consider it an opportunity for great joy. For you know that when your faith is tested, your endurance has a chance to grow. So, let it grow, for when your endurance is fully developed, you will be perfect and complete, needing nothing."

DETERMINATION

Kobe Bryant was one of the greatest professional basketball players of all time. However, it was a public moment of failure that forced him to develop renewed strength. As a rookie in 1997, he shot four embarrassing air balls to end the season against the Utah Jazz. They wrote about his shooting woes in every major paper. That failure ended up motivating him for a highly successful twenty-year career with the Los Angeles Lakers. Kobe Bryant's take on determination: "Once you know what failure feels like, determination chases success." Now, get ready to shoot that shot, get ready to get that promotion, and get ready to pay off your house in half the amount of time. You are in the process of becoming stronger and more successful because you were willing to risk it all and fall short.

Mindset: Do the work, give yourself time, and trust the process. This is where your strength is being developed!

WEEK 10

DO NOT MAKE DECISIONS IN ISOLATION

"You will never outperform your inner circle."

John Wooden

Draw close to God and He will connect you to the right team. God wants you to be humble and successful!

HOME TEAM

There is an immense amount of power in agreement. God is your ultimate source, the creator of every created thing. He has placed others around you to help you make important decisions, but how do you identify who those people are? There is only so much that other people can do for you, even when they mean well. God will come as far into your life as you will allow Him. As you build your home team, make sure you keep God in the center of it all. God is not confined to a building or a physical structure; He dwells in the agreement and unity of His people. In Matthew 18:19, Jesus said: "I also tell you this: If two of you agree here on earth concerning anything you ask, my Father in Heaven will do it for you."

WHAT DO YOU WANT?

Designate a set time each Monday morning to quietly connect with God's word and talk to Him about your dreams and goals. If you remain humble and trust Him with your plans, He will work every detail together for your good. You must intentionally seek out opportunities to practice the power of agreement. Always be mindful of your inner circle and remember that bad company corrupts good character. Life was not created to be done alone; your inner circle is there to help you make difficult decisions. You do not have to completely agree with everyone you meet, but you need to willingly listen to what others have to say and receive it wholeheartedly. Know what you want, stay connected, and have faith!

Mindset: Trust God, lean into your team, and believe strongly that the outcome will always be successful!

WEEK 11

POSITIVE MINDSET = POSITIVE OUTCOME

"You can't be a champion if you haven't been in a fight."

T.D. Jakes

You have been winning while you were losing because you were chosen. To remain positive in a difficult moment is easier said than done. Who you are now is not who you will be ten years from now!

IN DUE TIME

God will meet you in the work He has assigned you to do. He will not always bring you out of difficulties; sometimes He allows you to go through the process of coming through them. Jesus died for us, was placed in a tomb, and many of His disciples began to scatter. For three days, there were no witnesses, no crowds, no palm trees, and no singing of songs. If you truly want to walk with God, you must recognize your responsibility to step into the dark places and tombs of your dreams. Sooner or later, if you live long enough, you will experience a rough stretch of days like Jesus. John 17:4 says: "I brought glory to you here on earth by completing the work you gave me to do." The fight you are in is evidence of the extraordinary goodness God wants to bring into your life. There is a time to win and a time to lose. Everyday matters, and you must discipline your mind to remain positive before the fight begins. The people who do the greatest things in this life are those who function well in instability.

RESULTS

While everything is shaking, hold on to your faith. Learn how to have private problems in public places. Do not be shocked when it gets difficult; instead, be prepared for suffering. The season you are currently in is about to change. God picks His people, and He is already in your tomorrow. The outcome is simple: you already won!

Mindset: You do not necessarily know what tomorrow holds, but you can be confident in knowing that He holds tomorrow. Reset your mind and remain positive!

WEEK 12

SOW INTO YOUR VISION

"VISION will ignite the fire of passion that fuels our commitment to do WHATEVER IT TAKES to achieve excellence. Only VISION allows us to transform dreams of greatness into the reality of achievement through human action. VISION has no boundaries and knows no limits. Our VISION is what we become in life."

Tony Dungy

Never let them see you sweat. You are a leader who is surrounded with favor. Time to show up and show out!

BEYOND

Are you training yourself to see something beyond your current set of circumstances? Like a seed that goes into the ground and takes time to produce – so are your words. Many times, great vision requires that people must be willing to simply talk themselves into it. However, that is easier said than done, right? The problem many of us run into is that we do not recognize the power of our words. Steven Furtick: "If you have been told that God won't lead into difficult situations, you have been lied to."

YOU'RE NOT GOING THAT WAY

Human action is a requirement for God-sized dreams to become reality. Remember this, people will not lead if they do not read. You must read positive Scriptures, books, social media feeds, etc. Over, and over, and over again – read every day and then be ready to speak out what you took in. It takes strength and courage to speak things that are contrary to what you can see in the natural. In the book of Joshua, the Lord spoke to him first and then he spoke to the Israelites. They crossed the Jordan by following instructions. Chapter 3, verse 8: "Give this command to the priests who carry the Ark of the Covenant: 'When you reach the banks of the Jordan River, take a few steps into the river and stop there.'" The point is this: Joshua had to speak to the Israelites!

EYES FORWARD

Like Joshua, we all have Jericho's we are attempting to circle and seize in our lives. Jericho was a city that was tightly shut, a barrier between the people and a specific place. Take a moment to examine the team you have assembled and remember it is the people in your life who are most important. However, leaders must keep their eyes forward after they give directions, because they set the example for the team. Belief is a great starting point, but it is not enough. Your words are the seeds of your success. You cannot talk about defeat and have victory. Keep your mind positive. Keep a close grip on the words you speak. From the abundance of the human heart, your words will flow.

DIRECTION

You are about to accomplish the milestone. Know who you are, be willing to go the extra mile, and shout victory as you stare at your Jericho. What is your Jericho?

MINDSET: Get your head, heart, and words flowing in the same direction. Set the example for your team by talking yourself into it. You were made for greatness!

CLIMBING UP TAKES MUSCLE

"You have power over your mind – not outside events. Realize this, and you will find strength."

Marcus Aurelius

History shows time and time again that elevation is more of a developmental process than a straight-line trajectory. Regardless if you are a sports fan or not, many would agree that Coach Nick Saban is a strong leader.

BLOCKED PERSPECTIVE

Are you a glass half-empty or half-full kind of person? In today's microwave, instant success society, many people have lost their power over their mentality. Their mentality is simply their way of thinking. Are you a strong thinker or a weak thinker? Some lifestyle factors that impact mental health are as follows: exercise and activity level, dietary choices, relationships, meditation practices, and sleep habits. Between 1973 and 1989,

Saban served as an assistant coach for seven different universities. As a young coach, coming up the ranks, I would be willing to bet that he was a "both" kind of thinker. He thought outside the box, and he learned to appreciate the art of the climb. Andy Mineo: "They see you on the mountain, they don't see you on the climb." How many people who met Coach Saban during those fifteen years would have predicted how successful he would become as a head coach?

IT'S BOTH

I believe Saban realized his mind was a cup that needed to be both half-empty and half-full. Why? Because he realized early on that success requires movement. We all have hills and valleys in our lives, and if we are going to make it to the top consistently, we must learn to control the way we think. You cannot allow culture to dictate how you analyze the things outside of your control. Fill your glass with organized facts, simple rules, and processes. Then be willing to grow in knowledge by surrounding yourself with mentors and peers who challenge you. As you continue your climb up the mountain this week, be willing to alter your strategy to help you reach your highest potential. Your glass must not be sedentary or stale; it must be constantly evolving and working to become better at your craft.

INVEST YOUR TIME

Nick Saban: "When you invest your time, you make a goal and a decision of something that you want to accomplish. Whether it's make good grades in school, be a good athlete, be a good person, go down and do some community service and help somebody who's in need, whatever it is you choose to do, you're investing your time in that." Since 1973, Saban has invested his time in becoming the best coach he can be. If you will just keep showing up, you will be successful. If you will continue to sow good seeds and challenge yourself, you will be successful. The best things happen when you show up. Who needs you to be present today? Is it your family, your staff, your friends, that person you met online, a neighbor, etc.? Do not stop; keep going. You are close!

MINDSET: *"Let's not get tired of doing what is good. At just the right time we will reap a harvest of blessing if we do not give up." Galatians 6:9*

EMBRACE THE SUCK

"Pain is temporary. It may last for a minute, or an hour or a day, or even a year. But eventually, it will subside. And something else takes its place. If I quit, however, it will last forever."

Dr. Eric Thomas

Quitting is not an option, even if it has become normal in today's culture. You will not quit. Whatever you start, you must remain committed until it is finished.

N.O.W.

Do you think it is important to maximize your time each day, week, month, year? If so, then why? One thing all human beings have in common is the gift of time. It is one thing to think that maximizing your time is important, but it is another thing to truly believe it. What is the difference? Essentially, thoughts can occur in bunches. People literally think thousands of thoughts

34

each day. Believing is to hold onto something as true even though you have no definitive proof. For example, you can think you do not need to water your lawn because it rained earlier this morning – but you can believe the weather tomorrow will be perfect for a cookout. Simply defined, a belief is a confident faith that something will happen. Right now is the best time to embrace the discipline of making the most of your time. For the purpose of this week's Monday Mindset, the acronym N.O.W. represents Neurological Opportunities Win.

NEUROLOGICAL

The N. Neurology is the study of human nerves and the nerve system – as well as the diseases that impact them. Some examples of common neurological disorders are as follows: back pain, chronic fatigue syndrome, headaches and migraines, strokes, etc. There are many more! Why are we taking time today to examine the role of our neurological system? Because good health is real wealth. Your nervous system impacts all your everyday activities. Your breathing, emotions, thinking, and remembering. You can strengthen this system in your body through simple daily disciplines. Here are some practical examples: getting natural sunlight, meditation, exercise, drinking plenty of water, getting quality rest, limiting screen time, refraining from caffeinated beverages, etc. If you strengthen your mind, your body will follow.

OPPORTUNITIES

The O. Opportunities are all around, but are you ready for them when they come? If you are honest, that answer is usually no. A quick search on Google will reveal there is approximately one divorce in the United States every sixty seconds. Millions of young boys and girls register for youth sports every year, and more than half of them quit, to never play again, by the time they are in high school. Quitting becomes a habit. The rise of technology has become more than many people can handle. Life is so fast-paced, work-days have become extended, as the wall between work and home seems nonexistent. Learn to draw the line. Whether, it is turning your phone off at a certain hour of the evening, not allowing your child to quit that team, not giving up on your dream, or whatever that thing is for you – draw the line. Be ready when the opportu-nity comes and refuse to quit by embracing the climb up your ladder to success. Your greatest opportunities will often come through something or someone difficult. Embrace it!

WINNING

The W. To become a winner, you must learn how to use failure to push yourself to keep going, as opposed to giving up or quitting. Before Michael Jordan was ever a champion, he was a kid who was cut from his high school team and a man who was not named an NBA champion during his first six seasons in the league. Before David became king at thirty years old, he was a young boy who faced Goliath, as recorded in 1 Samuel 17:32: "Don't worry about this Philistine, David told Saul. I'll go fight him!" There will be someone or some-thing that will attempt to send doubt into your mind, just as Saul did to David in verse 33: "Don't be ridic-ulous! Saul replied. There's no way you can fight this

Philistine and possibly win! You're only a boy, and he's been a man of war since his youth."

Mindset: Do not take hardship as a sign that maybe you were not supposed to do it. Use your mind to view any difficulties or hardships as an opportunity for you to win. You are about to win. The time is right NOW!

WEEK 15

MILESTONES AND MEMORIES

"Remember to celebrate milestones as you prepare for the road ahead."

Nelson Mandela

L ook at how far you have come, and smile.

SHOW GRATITIDUE

To display gratitude is to show appreciation and thankfulness. What areas in your life have you become anxious about? To be anxious means to experience nervousness or worry about an event with an unknown outcome. When you want to achieve something badly enough, you can easily forget how far you have already come. One of the easiest ways to show others how grateful you are in your everyday life is to simply smile. Smile when it is good. Smile when it is bad. Smile no matter what, and when you cannot smile – then pray!

DO THIS INSTEAD

Philippians 4:6 says this: "Don't worry about anything; instead, pray about everything. Tell God what you need, and thank him for all he has done." Strong character and renewed mentalities are not things we inherit from our parents. Character and mentality must be built daily through our actions and decisions we make. We can choose to not worry by praying instead. This week pray periodically throughout the day – sometimes in a quiet place and other times within small moments without drawing attention to yourself. Make it simple by doing more listening than talking. I know you have a plan for your life, but you must trust that your best days are ahead and you have favor. You are in the middle of a memory-making season. I know you just finished something and are excited about the next thing on your list. However, I need you to slow down. Slow down, enjoy the journey, and always keep your mind positive. You have come so far already. The road ahead is ready for you once again!

MINDSET: With every milestone, learn to enjoy them!

TODAY'S SOUL VITAMINS

"Don't let the noise of others' opinions drown out your inner voice. And most important. Have the courage to follow your heart and intuition."

Steve Jobs

Every day matters. Each day is guided by the narrative you repeat in your head all day long. Are you being guided by a positive inner voice or a negative one?

BUILDING COURAGE

Humans must learn to be intentional about building and maintaining the foundation of their courage. The platform of your life is built on what you do with the concept of each day. You must learn to live in the moment, because you cannot control the future and you will never be able to rewind time. To be intentional, you must show up every day in ordinary moments like you were created to be there. You must empower yourself to pursue excellence. This can be done through the daily discipline of reading.

LEADERS ARE READERS

Faith comes by hearing, and the beauty of life is that we can choose the voices we listen to. Remember, we are urged to be quick to listen and slower to speak. To cultivate positive relationships within your community context, you must be willing to zoom out and see yourself from a different perspective. As you widen back the lens and look at the progression of your life, it becomes clear that words connect everything that can be seen with the human eye. Do you realize you should be reading something positive every single day? You cannot afford to take days off from reading or listening to meaningful messages. Leadership skills are sharpened through the discipline of daily reading. Albert Einstein likened an "intuitive mind" to that of a "sacred gift." Through reading each day, the mind becomes more instinctive and you will grow as a leader. If you do not remember anything else from this week, remember this: commit to being a lifelong learner.

THE FUNNY THING

When I first began reading the Bible, I thought I was reading it, but it was truly reading me. You are in the process of becoming instinctively excellent. You were created to be a bright light for others to see. You were created to set the example with your life's work. You are smart. You are amazing. You are a leader. By reading every day, you will boost your intellect, lower stress, strengthen relationships, sleep better, and have a good reason to put that cellphone down. Do not forget what you look like. James 1:22-24 MSG says it like this: "Don't fool yourself into thinking that you are a listener when you are anything but, letting the Word go in one ear and out the other. Act on what you hear! Those who hear and don't act are like those who glance in the mirror, walk away, and two minutes later have no idea who they are, what they look like." Today, make sure you take your Soul Vitamins and courageously control your inner voice.

MINDSET: Soul Vitamins = God's Eternal Word

THE KOBE BRYANT FACTOR

"I don't want to be the next Michael Jordan, I only want to be Kobe Bryant."

Kobe Bryant

ou do not need to try to be anyone else!

BE YOURSELF

Have you ever been so close you could see what was possible, but you could not get all the way to it? We must learn to deal with the feelings of uncertainty. Get this thought in your spirit: you are a winner and you are enough. If your dreams do not frighten you, then they are simply too small. You were not created to live a boring and safe life. Without the risk of failure, embarrassment, and uncertainty, there is no reward that will truly fulfill your desires. Quit pointing out problems and develop the ability to create solutions. Face the day, fight for your dreams, and live life like today is your last day on earth. Expect good things to happen in your life.

DON'T SHORT-CHANGE

It is very dangerous to have low expectations. When you do not expect much, you are not fully utilizing the ability of your mind. Expect that your life is worthy of greatness. Kobe Bryant believed that the things we say out of our mouths, especially regarding failure, can short-change our lives. We must dare to fail. We must dare to be different. We must dare to be ourselves and not get trapped in comparison. Comparison will steal your joy. Trade in comparison for conviction. Conviction is a firmly held belief or opinion. Be convicted that it is okay to fail, because you will not allow the failure to make you quit. Be convicted that you are courageous in the face of adversity. Be convicted that your best days are ahead of you. Be convicted that you have greatness within you; the kind of greatness that will impact the lives of other people long after you are gone. Never allow a negative thought to come directly out of your mouth. You will have thoughts of comparison and doubt, but learn to correct them early and often!

THE UNSEEN

Hebrews 11:1 says: "Now faith is the assurance of things hoped for, the conviction of things not seen." God is aligning your life with favorable outcomes. There is a shift headed your way. In basketball, you miss every shot you are unwilling to take. In baseball, you swing and miss when you take your eyes off the ball. Consistency is rewarded over enough time. Kobe Bryant played twenty seasons for one NBA franchise, the Los Angeles Lakers. Have you put in enough time to master your craft? Have you taken inventory of your thoughts? Have you envisioned yourself reaching that milestone? Have you become more focused on what you can see over what you cannot? The door to your future will open at the right time. A seed will sprout and begin to rapidly grow in its time. You have an appointed time to achieve what you are working toward. Sometimes it just takes time and consistency. Your faithfulness will be rewarded.

MINDSET: Set the bar high and aim for the stars. You will learn that your mentality is the X-factor in your life. You have everything you need, and you will win. Not by being someone else, but by simply being you!

FOCUS ON YOUR HEALTH

"Mental health…is not a destination, but a process. It's about how you drive, not where you're going."

– Noam Shpancer, PhD

Where your focus goes, your energy will follow. You may be standing at the edge of the waters, but you are going to the other side – learn to control your focus.

THE BODY

Do you have the courage to get better? Do you have the desire to control your physical strength and endurance? To be prepared for what God is about to do in your life, you must get in shape. Physical fitness is a life-long process, where you must make weekly deposits. Do you have a running or walking routine? Do you work on your core? Is your health a top priority in your life? If you do not have health and happiness on the inside, you will never have it externally. Remember, comparison is the thief of joy. Focus on being the best you can be each day by developing routines you enjoy and mastering them. Make time to invest in your body every day. Pray, train, conquer, repeat. The way your body feels matters!

THE HEART

Your heart will beat over 100,000 times today. Each year, heart disease is the leading cause of death in the United States; about 25 percent of all deaths for both men and women. The health of your heart deserves your attention. Some effective ways to strengthen your heart are as follows: get moving every day, refrain from smoking, meal planning, and regular cardiovascular training. The Bible says something profound about the heart in Proverbs 4:23: "Above all else, guard your heart, for everything you do flows from it." You must be intentional about using your gift. God never creates a soul without giving that person a gift. You are gifted and your gift will flow directly out of the things you treasure in your heart. Make sure your heart is always in a healthy place. Your focus is the doorkeeper to all your thinking.

THE MIND

Focus on what is working in your life, not on what is not working. The enemy in your life is trying to distract you by getting you to think about what is not working. Most people prefer to make excuses rather than make an adjustment. The anatomy of your brain is divided into two hemispheres. To simplify my point, you have an "I can do it" and an "I cannot do it" hemisphere in your mind. When you learn to control your thoughts, you gradually become tough-minded. You become strong and determined about things that used to keep you in the "cannot" hemisphere. Persistence in the face of failure and loss is evident in tough-minded people. You were born to succeed. Your thoughts become words and words exit your body through your mouth. You will conquer your assignment by realizing your success is within your control. Strive daily to become more tough-minded!

THE SPIRIT

If you will devote what you are doing to better the next generation, it will always bear fruit. This week, make sure the example you set exudes character, confidence, and courage.

MINDSET: *Maximize your body, heart, mind, and spirit.*

CLIMB THE HILL

"You've gotta be hungry."

Les Brown

The lion on the hill is never as hungry as the lion climbing the hill. Master the climb and remain hungry.

RESPONSIBILTY

You were put on this planet to do something great. At this very moment, there are leadership skills developing within you. To be a great leader is not an easy thing. There are many people who admire leadership, but they are not ready for the challenges and responsibilities that come tied to it. No one wants to hear what you have been through – they only want to hear that you got the job done. What is your assignment? Lock in on what it is and just do it. Ownership is key. It is important to know that you are stronger while climbing the hill than you are once you have made it to the top.

THE LION

Every decision you make will have a domino effect. Whether you recognize it or not, the God of all creation is building your resume. You may feel unqualified or unworthy, but that is not true. You cannot be certain where or when the seeds of your faith will experience evident growth, but if you will be faithful right where you are and continue to climb, God will bless you. The roar of a lion can be heard from over four miles away. You must shout your way to success. It will happen. I cannot see it yet, but I know it will certainly happen. I do not know how but I do know who. The reality is if God laid out the entire journey at your feet, you would run away from it or despise the climb. Loved one, do not despise the day of small beginnings. The hill you are climbing will be worth it. The dominos are beginning to fall in the right direction. Keep soaring, keep running, keep walking, crawl if you must. Whatever you do is going to prosper!

MINDSET: You are about to overcome your obstacle!

ALLIGNMENT MATTERS

"Show me your friends and I'll show you
your future."

Mark Ambrose

You need three types of people in your life. People
who inspire you, people who hold you accountable,
and people whom you help lead in a better direction.

INSPIRATION

Being around other human beings is just as contagious as secondhand smoke, so you must intentionally
align yourself with good people. There are thousands of
cancer-causing chemicals that flow into the atmosphere
from the burning end of a cigarette or cigar. Inspiration
is similar to secondhand smoke, because it is through
the process of mental stimulation that you become
creatively brilliant. Do the people you spend the most
time with inspire you to live an extraordinary life or
not? Your ideas matter. If you do not surround yourself
with caring, disciplined, enthusiastic, innovative, and

trustworthy people, you will not be inspired to have victorious thoughts. Your thoughts are the genesis point for millions of possible great victories. Get around other people who inspire you to walk with purpose in every step. Start developing a vision of victory for your life. As you begin to envision where you want to be five, ten or fifteen years from now, understand that your relationships largely impact your future. Build your inner circle with people who build you up continuously and love pouring into you.

ACCOUNTABILTY

You must have balance in your life. Are you prepared for God to balance the weight in your life? You must admit that the weights of this world are too heavy for one person to carry alone. You cannot move into the places God wants to move you into if you do not distribute the weight. Like a college or professional sports team with aspirations to win a championship, it will not happen if the weight always falls on one person. Having people in your life who not only listen to you when you need an ear, but also tell you things that are hard to hear, is an invaluable thing. 1 Thessalonians 5:11 says this: "Therefore encourage one another and build one another up, just as you are doing." Alone, you cannot handle what God wants to do through your life. To be accountable to another human involves accepting responsibility for things that should be done anyway. We are the greatest versions of ourselves when we are on our A-game, even when no one is watching. When you make a mistake in an area of your life, take it to someone you trust and let them be your accountability partner. You need a judgment-free relationship in your life. You need someone to tell you that you were wrong, but it will be okay. You have the passion, the heart, and the gifting for what you are trying to accomplish in this life, but you must have some help. Take a moment to consider who that person is in your life and talk to them every week. We are better at balancing the weight in our lives when we are being held accountable and not doing life alone!

GO THIS WAY

Good leadership is always fruitful. Whether you realize it or not, you are a leader. Are you leading others into a better direction? Are you trying to micromanage others to get what you want out of life? Be a strong enough leader that you are not intimidated by people because they are not like you in every area. Just because they do not think like you does not mean someone is wrong. Choosing to follow Jesus requires answering the call to discipleship. You cannot love God and hate others. You are in position to make a tremendous impact on each person around you. Get this in your head: your life is a story created to teach eternal truths. Accept responsibility for the storm you are currently in and be ready for the opportunity to teach. Teaching is simply showing someone else the way. This week, you are going to be presented with opportunities to lead the people in your life in a positive direction. If you remain rooted in God's word, you will illuminate the way for others. Jesus used parables, which are short stories designed to illustrate or teach eternal truths. In Matthew, Jesus spoke about building on solid foundations. He gave the illustration of two people who built a house on different foundations, one on sand and one on rock. Matthew 7:28-29 says: "When Jesus had finished saying these things, the crowds were amazed at his teaching, for he taught with real authority – quite unlike their teachers of religious law."

MINDSET: *Your future and friendships are one and the same. You have permission to align yourself with the right people. Do you know which way to go from here?*

MAINTAIN YOUR MOMENTUM

"Momentum solves 80 percent of your problems."

John C. Maxwell

Be where your feet are, and you will stay on track.

RAILROAD TRACKS

Mass multiplied by velocity equals momentum. Your mindset headed into this week represents your mass. Your velocity is how fast you are going in a specific direction. What direction are you headed this week and how fast are you going to get there? Your mind is like a train that is firmly placed on a set of railroad tracks. Success and hard work run parallel to each other, and you cannot gain meaningful momentum without both. Wooden railroads were created in the United States during the early 1700s. They played a major role in the development of the U.S. Powered by either steam, diesel, or electricity, trains are powerful tools that can be used to carry heavy loads over great distances in record time. A train without a track will not reach its desired destination. If you do not get your thinking on the right track, you will be slowed down to a complete stop. What is your track?

PROBLEMS

There is nothing more powerful than a changed mind and this world is starving for solution-oriented people. If you think you can, you probably will. You will naturally become solution oriented by never quitting something you start. Like every human, you will face problems this week, some expected and others unexpected. Use seeds to overcome your problems. A seed cannot be used if it is not planted and given enough time to grow. Are you planting enough seeds into your heart and mind? Acts 19:20 says: "So the word of the Lord grew mightily and prevailed." Our words, the things we say out of our mouths, are the vehicles for maintaining enough velocity to run over life's problems. God's word will keep you on track. Before you do anything today, change what you believe is possible!

MINDSET: When things come against you this week, do not allow yourself to become overwhelmed – instead, speak faith to it. Momentum flows from the mouth!

FLAWED BUT FRUITFUL

"Perfection is not attainable, but if we chase perfection, we can catch excellence."

Vince Lombardi

Get it out of your head that you must be perfect.

EVIDENCE

Those who insist on living within their comfort zone miss out on their growth phase. Is there not a great cost associated with your call to leadership? Your greatest opportunities will knock on the door during chaos. It is through highly chaotic moments that you can become a conqueror. The more outside pressure is applied, the more the internal greatness begins to emerge. You do not know what type of abilities you have if you do not go through hard times. In our minds, we often think that we must do everything the right way on the first try – not true. In what areas of your life are you already bearing good fruit and being successful? Use that evidence to focus on the good in your life. You might make mistakes, but you are already making tremendous progress.

MESSY BUSINESS

What are you chasing? A college degree, job, spouse, business accomplishment, sports championship – we are all chasing something. Your mind is like a magnet: the things you choose to focus on will become attracted to your life. If you choose to focus on the mistakes you have made, then you will make those same mistakes more often. If you choose to focus on your blessings, then you will appreciate how far you have already come on your success journey. If you focus on who left you, you will miss out on enjoying the people who are still in your life. If you focus on being prepared for opportunities, you will be ready to conquer them when they surface in your life. The truth is like a beach ball held under water: no matter how hard you try to suppress it, it will eventually reach the surface. Here is the truth: life is messy, but God is turning your mess into His masterpiece. What are you attracting in your mess?

THE TREE

To be fruitful is to produce good, helpful, and productive results. Your life is like a tree and it is always producing something. Do you meditate? If not, I encourage you to start. Focus your mind for a duration of time, in silence, for spiritual and relaxation purposes. Mentally plan a strategy for your life so you will respond greatly in chaos. There is tremendous value within learning how to live wisely. So much wisdom can be found within the first three verses of Psalm 1 in the Bible. It says:

"Blessed is the one who does not walk in step with the wicked or stand in the way that sinners take or sit in the company of mockers, but those whose delight is in the law of the Lord, and who meditates on his law day and night. That person is like a tree planted by streams of water, which yields fruit in season and whose leaf does not wither – whatever they do prospers." Chase after perfection but let go of the idea that you will obtain it. If you steward your time, talent, and treasure appropriately, you will be successful in everything you do. Take that to the bank.

MINDSET: Be willing to let go of your definition of success and trade that thought in for God's plan.

STAY IN THE ARENA

"It is not the critic who counts; not the man who points out how the strong man stumbles, or where the doer of deeds could have done them better. The credit belongs to the man who is actually in the arena, whose face is marred by dust and sweat and blood; who strives valiantly."

Theodore Roosevelt

You have just enough time and energy remaining within you to make the rest of your life the best of your life.

WHAT YOU DON'T HAVE

Why are you counting what you do not have, when you should be laser focused on what you do have? You do not have time to play games and take a single day for granted. You cannot allow the noise from critical people to overpower your ability to control and renew your thoughts each day. It is your responsibility to control your inner narrative and to stick to the plan.

THERE IS A PLAN

Words to remember from the prophet Jeremiah 29:11 promises: "For I know the plans I have for you," say the Lord. "They are plans for good and not for disaster, to give you a future and a hope." It is imperative that we hold on to the promises of God found in Scripture. Any significant accomplishment always requires us to invest a lot of our time and is process-based. A process can be defined as a series of actions that produce something or lead to a particular result. We must learn to work with joy and patience – these things help us to remember the promises. For every promise, you will face a problem.

TRIALS COME ATTACHED

The trials we face and the toughest moments in our lives are the very tools God uses to create within us a champion's mentality. We have all been created to shine bright, to fill the earth with God's glory, and to live a life filled with love. Why do the trials come so often if this is true? Because we are in the process of being fully developed and there is a plan. Trees are great examples for us to learn from. When the fall time comes and a tree is about to die, the leaves turn many bright colors: orange, red and yellow. Afterward, they fall off the tree and die; for months, trees remain bare and without any leaves. Once the spring comes around, they become renewed and restored naturally. Hear what I am saying clearly: God has a process and His plan always works. When you face anxiety, adversity, or any kind of undesirable situation, count it as joy, because you will bounce back stronger and more vibrant than before.

A WORD FROM JAMES

James addressed his audience as "dear brothers and sisters." This shows he cared for many diverse groups of people who would hear his message long after he was gone. He challenged us to count it as joy, which is easier said than done, but is also something we can do if we stay in the arena. You have staying power. Stay at that job. Stay in that marriage. Stay encouraging people who need it. Stay doing the right thing while no one is watching. God will reward you, but that part will come after your test. Whatever your arena is, stay in it! James 1:2 says this: "Dear brothers and sisters, when troubles of any kind come your way, consider it an opportunity for great joy. For you know that when your faith is tested, your endurance has a chance to grow." Remember these steps as you begin running into the week ahead: do not focus on what you do not have. He has a great plan for your life, trials and tests are part of the plan, and you can find joy with the right mentality.

KEEP COMPETING

Anyone can stand outside the arena and criticize you for your faults, but it takes true power to stay in it.

MINDSET: Take a deep breath and simply focus on the things you can control in your life. Your mindset is one of them and you are stronger than you originally thought. Strength does not come from what we could already do, but from

overcoming difficult things we could not do. It is time to go conquer your arena!

WEEK 24

LOVE ME FOR FREE

"Life's most persistent and urgent question is, "What are you doing for others?"

Dr. Martin Luther King Jr.

our feelings and your faith are two separate things.

FEELINGS

Feelings can be simply defined as an emotional state or reaction to something. Who cleans the house where you live? The floors, the kitchen counters, and the toilets must be cleaned regularly. Most of us were given an outline of what household cleaning and maintenance looks like from our parents and family members. In one home, the mother may do all the laundry, the dishes, cook the food, clean toilets, etc. That example can carry over for generations, but is it really a woman's job to always do the dishes, cook the food, and clean the dirty places of the house? In John 13, Jesus washed the stinking feet of His disciples. He did this to give us an example and demonstrate that people should be willing to go above and beyond for others. In a practical way, how can you wash someone else's feet this week?

FAITH

Do it anyway. When no one will notice your efforts to do something small in a great way, do it anyway. Faith can simply be defined as complete trust or confidence in someone. You do not always have to feel like doing something to do it in faith. Faith is not a feeling. Faith is a mentality that, regardless of the outcome or what you can get out of a situation for doing something, you will do it anyway. Faith is living your life in a way that considers others as more important than yourself. We all need jobs; jobs are good things, and they provide us with a source of income and responsibility. However, you must never confuse your job with your work.

JOBS vs WORK

Hear this clearly: your work is what you were born to do. Your thoughts matter. Instead of feeling like "I cannot do it," try saying, "I can do all things through Christ." Instead of feeling like "I have to do it," try saying, "I get to do it." Coach yourself up and be the captain of your thoughts. You will experience feelings, but this is the very place your faith muscles can go to work. You are a world changer. You are powerful. You are amazing. Your work is about to make a major impact this week because you have favor. Let me give you a new definition of favor – it is when God breaks the rules to bless you. Your blessings will be found in the simple acts of doing kind and honorable things for others. Even if you do not feel like it, do it anyway. How can you apply this lesson and accelerate the favor in your life this week?

MINDSET: You must be willing to do things for someone else without expecting anything in return. When you learn to master this skill, the people God has strategically placed in your life will love you for free!

WEEK 25

SET THE EXAMPLE

"A good example has twice the value of good advice."

Albert Schweitzer

Whatever it takes.

QUIT WORRYING

Why do you keep rehearsing that thing in your head repeatedly? Thinking about things is okay, but when you think about something five or more times, it becomes worry. Worried about paying your bills on time. Worried about everyone liking every decision you make. Worried about something you saw on the news. Worried about the person who walked away from your life. Worry must be addressed immediately and overcome with the power of a sound mind. Your mind is yours and the things you choose to focus on will determine your inner narrative. As humans, it is easy to get caught up in the routine of worry. Here is some great news: you are not God, you are only human, and you do not have to have all the answers. 2 Timothy 1:7 tells us this: "For God has not given us a spirit of fear and timidity, but of power and of love and of a sound mind."

EXPECT CHATTER

When something amazing is about to occur in your life, you will begin to recognize the chatter. Recognizing the chatter is fine, but accepting it as true impacts your drive toward your purpose in life. What is chatter? Chatter is the act of talking rapidly about trivial matters. People will talk when you are doing good and they will talk when you are doing bad – so let them. Receive this into your spirit before you go any further this week: people who function at a highly successful level do not have time to chatter, so if they are chattering about you in a negative way it is probably because they are bored, jealous, or both. Your value does not come from what you say or what they say, it comes from what you do. Do not let the noise stop you from your next breakthrough. Block it out and focus on how you can continue to set a good and honorable example in your community. What is a breakthrough? It is a sudden, dramatic, and important development in your life. Hear this clearly – your blessings are going to come suddenly! However, they will not come to pass if you get distracted by naysayers chattering about you in a negative way. Are you ready for a major change in some area of your life? If you are going to break through to your next level, it will come at a great cost. It may cost you money, friendships, time, etc. Once you have moved past worry, the next step is to develop a mentality that is willing to pay the cost. The question then becomes: Are you willing to pay that cost?

THE START

The most dangerous thing you can lose in life is your faith. Dare to dream so big that it frightens you. Dare to overcome adversity by embracing the hard times. Dare to accomplish something so great that you have no reference point for how it will eventually happen. Dare to use your mind as the vehicle of faith to drive you across the highway of constant change. Remember that breakthroughs are sudden and the greatest blessings in your life will come faster than you could naturally expect. Are you becoming stronger while you wait? Are you putting in the time necessary to master your life's work? Just because it did not start the way you would have planned it does not mean it will not end in success. Do not just go through adverse circumstances, grow through them. Continue to go to work, raising your children, making that purchase, applying for that position, enrolling in higher education, etc. God has placed people in your life who are watching you, and you must remain focused on the finish.

YOUR AUDIENCE

If you knew every detail from beginning to end, you probably would never have started that thing you are working on. Do not wait for a major change to occur without strengthening yourself daily. You must become stronger while you wait. Your life is meant to inspire faith in the people around you. You cannot lead if you will not read. Reading is a discipline and words make the world go around. What words are you listening to and focusing on as you run your race? Does your audience see you on your A-game when you face adversity?

How can you improve this week to positively impact those around you? How can you make a difference? How can you be the change they need? Somehow or another, down in your spirit, you know something great is about to happen. Maintain your momentum no matter what!

THE FINISH

Do not be afraid of disappointment. Disappointment is not the end of your race, so keep running. Your faith is only developed as you learn to finish. We live in a generation of quitting and not finishing what we started. Not you. No matter what, your mindset is slowly becoming: I will finish this. Change is inevitable and your future is filled with positive change. Just because you do not see it does not mean anything. The greatest progress is often accelerated during seasons of waiting. Keep hoping you will finish strong. Keep trusting that your steps were ordered long before you were born. Hebrews 11:1 tells us: "Now faith is the assurance of things hoped for, the conviction of things not seen." No matter what type of adversity or change comes in your direction this week, you will overcome it. Keep your expectations high and set the example with your actions every day.

MINDSET: Disappointment is only possible where expectation is present. Never minimize your expectations. Keep them extremely high and trust that strong character will make you invaluable to the world.

WEEK 26

POSITIVE ENTHUSIASM

"I'm gonna make the rest of my life the
best of my life."

Dr. Eric Thomas

Move forward enthusiastically and remain positive.

NECESSARY

Forgetting is a necessary component in moving forward. Potential is a great tool we have been given that
lights a fire in us to become something greater than we
currently are. However, your time is up from the last
season and it is time for you to get moving. You must
remain positive during your time in transition. A transition is simply the space between where you were and
where you are going. Potential is having or showing the
capacity to become or develop into something great in
the future. The rest of your life starts today; you must
unleash yourself from doubt and learn how to maximize the twenty-four. There are only twenty-four hours
in a day and your success is dependent upon how you

71

use your time. Forget where you were and move forward to where you are going.

CURRENT LOCATION

When you fail in some area of your life, go through those moments with a smile on your face. This is easier said than done, but it is certainly possible with a positive mindset. Giving teaches us how to have faith, and faith provides us with a sense of direction. During your seasons of transition, you will experience the reality of pain. The twenty-four hours ahead of you may not be easy, but you are strong enough to give today your all. If you are willing to give it, it will be given to you. Use the gifts you were given by God to create a positive impact in your community. It is okay to fail, just do not stay stuck there.

THE PRINCIPLE OF GIVING

The decision has already been made; you want to be the best version of yourself. If you thought there was no room for improvement, then you would not have picked up this book. Luke 6:38 says this: "Give, and it will be given to you. A good measure, pressed down, shaken together and running over." Give your mind to God's word and the blessings will begin to overflow abundantly in your life. Adjusting your mentality from getting to giving takes time and routine, but it is a routine you will learn to enjoy. As you transition from your potential to your next level, embrace the gift of giving to others. Send that encouraging text. Write that thank you letter. Buy that person a coffee. Send the flowers. Make an investment in someone else and it will always come back to you. Giving is a biblical principle that has stood the test of time. I dare you to apply if to your life this week!

MINDSET: *You never know who needs your smile, your kind words, and your positive demeanor. Let your life bring positive enthusiasm to your community today!*

ESTABLISH THE PATTERN

> "Character cannot be developed in ease and quiet. Only through experience of trial and suffering can the soul be strengthened, ambition inspired, and success achieved."

Helen Keller

Your future is totally dependent upon your character.

TRIAL AND SUFFERING

Your charm, gifting, talents, and passion will not protect you from trials and suffering. If you are going to make it through the toughest seasons in your life, you are going to need to develop self-discipline. Self-discipline leads to strong moral principles. People of strong character do not need to do a lot of talking – they simply need to show up. Why is that? The most effective leaders do not lead with persuasive language; instead, they lead with their lives. Are you ready to be a more effective leader? You must develop and maintain an unwavering level of character. Your words, your deeds, and your actions must all be united. People will follow your lead if they feel like they can trust you. How can you earn their trust? Be consistent in your dedication to a very high set of standards without wavering. When you do not waver in the middle of a test, it produces character, and that ultimately attracts their loyalty.

YOUR PATTERN

Did you know that everyone was created to lead in some area of life? A pattern is a model or design that can be used as a guide. In life, you cannot quit because you are experiencing a difficult season – although many people do. Effective leaders with strong character need a guide to navigate the struggles of leadership. Let me encourage you to allow this verse from Ecclesiastes to speak into your heart and mind today. Chapter 3, verse 1 tells us this: "For everything there is a season." There is a time to give and a time to receive. There is a time to get a job and a time to get fired or move on from that job. There is a time to laugh and a time to cry. As humans, we cannot see the entire scope of what God is doing in our day. However, the seasons we go through give us some clues toward where we are going and reminders of how far we have already come. People with strong character do not live according to what is popular – they live by their principles. The patterns in your life will lead you directly to your principles. Make sure you are living right and holding yourself to the highest standard.

CULTURE

Culture has trained us to get a job and not to find our gift. Your gifts are capable of inspiring others and that inspiration can be very contagious. Do you know what your gifts are? Write them down and keep them in plain sight this week. Did you know every human will be held accountable by God for the gifts and talents they have been given? With that in mind, I must emphasize that your character is what ultimately protects your future. As you begin to examine what is next in your life, you must realize that you must be tough enough to outlast the seasons. You are not a quitter. Instead, you lead with your character. Remember, experience is the only way you will develop strong character. I do not know what kind of season you are currently experiencing, but I do know there is a season for everything. Would you throw away your summer clothes because fall has arrived, and you know winter is right around the corner? No, you certainly would not!

ACHIEVEMENT

Have faith that spring and summer will come back around. Be confident your best days are always ahead of you. Trust that better circumstances will be here sooner, rather than later. Why? Because you have established an honorable pattern in your life. Every season you experience is like patterns for you to follow, knowing things will come back around in a certain direction – at the right time! One of the most important requirements for sustained success is strong character. You were created for a specific purpose and you are about to experience great success. How do I know this? Because you can be confident in this: the greater the suffering, the greater the success. Your future is bright!

MINDSET: Empty yourself enough to receive the character God wants to develop in your life. Be committed to living a life of strong character that overcomes the trials and suffering of today's times.

WEEK 28

WORK IT ALL TOGETHER

> "There will be obstacles. There will be doubters. There will be mistakes. But with hard work, there are no limits."
>
> *Michael Phelps*

What is ahead of you is always more than what is behind you. The thing that connects your past to the future you want is your ability to work as hard as you possibly can. Keeping your mind straight requires work!

OBSTACLES

Are you ready to go from valley to victory? Then you must understand that you must overcome the obstacle in front of you. Each day brings a variety of challenges, but one thing is for sure – you can only take things one step at a time. Your mind is a like a spear. A spear is a weapon with a long, pointed tip, usually made with hard stone or metal, used for thrusting, or throwing. As you move forward this week, you have got

78

to throw your mind at your obstacles. Victory begins with a thought. You are only one thought away from a new reality. You are one thought away from the life you want. Have faith in your ability to overcome and patiently endure the roads to success. Whatever obstacles may come your way – yes, you can. No matter how hard it looks – yes, you can. If it seems impossible – yes, you can. You must read daily, listen to podcasts, and surround yourself with positive people to remain sharp. Your mind is the tip of the spear!

DOUBTERS AND MISTAKES

Just because you are aware of the existence of doubters and mistakes does not mean you are not headed in the right direction. Who told you that you had to be perfect? Who told you that worry was an effective weapon? You must know your priorities are stronger than anything a doubter can ever say about you. Your priorities will bring order into your daily life. Your priorities are the things you spend the most time on. Your priorities are the things that will carry you through any mistake you make along the way. The creator of heaven and earth worked six days to create all the things we see before resting on the seventh. What creativity have you allowed to go dormant in your job? Give today your all, work hard, and do everything with joy. Working hard is a good and honorable thing.

NO LIMITS

One of the greatest promises in the Bible can be found in Romans 8:28. It says: "And we know that God causes everything to work together for the good of those who love God and are called according to his purpose for them." It does not say *we think*, it clearly says *we know*. Be confident that limits do not apply to you. Believe it is possible. You will pay that debt off. You will make a positive difference in the lives of the people all around you this week. You will make your family proud. You will be the hardest-working person in the room. You will keep moving forward and you will inspire greatness.

MINDSET: Expect things to work out in your favor. Take everything that happens to you and respond in faith. Remain patient, keep your mind sharp, do not worry, and remove the limitations in your mind. Yes, you can!

NEVER FORGET HOW YOU STARTED

"Remember why you started, remember where you're headed, think of how great it will be when you get there, and keep going."

Ralph Marston

o not despise the day of small beginnings.

YOUR TIME

Did you know God's number one key to success in your life is management? An extreme amount of power lies within how you manage your time. The earth is filled with resources and management is the very tool you can use to attract them. One way to maximize your time each week is through the process of review and renew. You must examine why you want to accomplish something and what the beginning stages looked like. It may seem small right now, but renew your mindset to focus on how big it will become. Let us take a moment to reflect on the importance of a foundation. A foundation can be described as the lowest load-bearing part of a building, usually beneath the ground level. Have you been spending too much time on one area of your life? Is it possible you have not been spending enough time on another area? Take a moment to review your time spent and make sure you prioritize it well. Once you have renewed the foundation of your mind, you are ready for the next phase of building your dreams.

YOUR TREASURE

In Matthew 6, Jesus says something profound. It is found in verse 21: "For where your treasure is, there your heart will also be." I would like to challenge you to give God the first part of everything you own: your paycheck, your marriage, your job, your relationships with your neighbors, etc. If you will do this, you will show God you are developing into a more effective manager whom He can trust with more. Right now, can you properly manage what He wants to give you? What things do you treasure the most in your life? If you have never written them down on paper and numbered them from greatest to least, I urge you to do so now. Take a moment and ask yourself, "What do I value the most?" and put it on paper. If you give someone money as a gift for their birthday, you are giving them a piece of your heart. If you give someone your time, helping them paint the insides of an old school building, you are giving them a piece of your heart. If you bet money on professional sporting events, you are giving them a piece of your heart. How you manage your time and your treasure determines the level of triumph you will see when you get to your desired destination.

YOUR TRIUMPH

You must stay focused on where you are going. You must recognize your strengths and weaknesses and remain patient with yourself. You must learn how to pace yourself in the race of life. What is a pace and how do you learn it? A pace is a single step taken while walking or running. It can also be described as consistent speed during movement. Begin the work required to continue the progress you have already made. Begin the work to embed in your mind how great it will be when you arrive. Begin the work of being accountable to yourself for the time and treasure you were given. Zechariah 4:10 says this: "Do not despise these small beginnings, for the Lord rejoices to see work begin." Every day, you are responsible for making a deposit in the life you are building. Every day, you must renew your mind to remain focused on God's number one key to your success. Right now, before you begin this week, plan to successfully manage everything in your life. Recognize this: whatever you fail to manage well, you will ultimately lose. Remembering this, God will always give more blessings to His effective stewards. A great victory or achievement is on the way. It is time for you to triumph over this week!

MINDSET: Go to Matthew 25 and read the parable of the three servants. Take some notes and apply what you take away from the story to your life this week. Surely, you will show yourself faithful over few!

DOORWAYS AND DESTINY

"It's better to be prepared for an opportunity and not have one, than to have an opportunity and not be prepared."

Les Brown

Do the work of preparation and the details of your success will take care of themselves at the right time.

PREPARATION

Would you go to an interview without doing your research on the business or organization? Would you play a football game without an offseason of practice? If you knew today was the greatest opportunity of your life, would you go into it unprepared? An opportunity is simply a set of circumstances that makes it possible to accomplish something great. Get it in your head right now that you will be prepared whenever that opportunity comes your way this week. Success may look easy to the spectator, but every detail matters. Greatness requires accepting responsibility for your own future. A successful future is birthed in your thoughts.

DETAILS

You must develop and maintain a weekly process of strengthening your mind. The world will naturally cause you to feel fatigued if you are chasing a dream that is worthwhile. One of the most important things to remember while chasing success in the field of life is this: worry is not an effective weapon. Never worry. Instead, keep yourself busy by focusing on the details of your life. Make up your bed before you leave the house. Iron the wrinkles out of that shirt. Keep your sink free of excessive dirty dishes. Make eye contact while talking to that business partner. Keep watch over everything under your possession and supervision. If you will be faithful with what you have, God will be excited to give you more. Therefore, you should aim to be detail-oriented in everything you do. The Bible says it like this in 1 Corinthians 14:40: "Let all things be done decently and in order." Being detail-oriented is a mindset and it is something that you must work on. You are exactly what you believe. What thoughts are playing in your mind?

DOORWAYS

As you walk out the door today, remind yourself of these positive truths. You are amazing. You are strong. You are on your way to success. The door that closed had a purpose. The door that will soon open is greater than you can imagine. The narrative you allow to play within your mind is extremely powerful. Your life is setting a standard for others to see and you should never take this lightly. Focus on being great at whatever you do. Recognize that your mentality is like an operating system in your life. The strength of your system will determine how long it takes you to reach your destiny. You must remain ready when the door opens. Readiness begins in your mind before manifesting itself in your life. Stay ready!

MINDSET: Your work matters. No matter what you do, your work is attached to your destiny. What God has for you is only for you. Each door takes you one step closer!

WEEK 31

DO NOT STOP ON SIX

"You are responsible for how people remember you, or don't. So don't take it lightly."

Kobe Bryant

Right after Moses died, it was time for Joshua to lead the way. Leading the way develops your character and ultimately determines the level of responsibility you are ready to manage. We must not take a single day God gives us for granted. Make a list of seven obstacles currently in your way. Tape them up on your mirror and circle them daily with your commitment and consistency.

STOPPING TAKES MUCH LONGER

Any time you are working hard to accomplish anything worthwhile in your life you will face great adversity. Joshua 6:1 gives us a great image of the obstacles we will face in our lives, even today: "Now the gates of Jericho were tightly shut because of the Israelites. No one was allowed in or out." Your dream may seem like it has come to an unmovable stopping point but remember this: your mind will try to deceive you. Whether you realize it or not, you have a Jericho. Your Jericho is the location you currently inhabit. Before you go any further this week, it is critical that you identify your Jericho and put it on paper. It is okay to slow down, rest, and reflect – but do not stop and stay in that place for too long. See James 1:1-7 for further instructions!

HALFTIME

How can you fail if you have already won? The only way you can fail is if you do not keep the right thoughts in your mind. You have the greatest coach of all time on your side. The Creator of heaven and earth is whose team you play for. God is not only your Heavenly Father, but He is also your coach. He will always lead you to success if you are willing to change the way you play. Be willing to review, revise, and reset your vision. Does it align with His purpose for your life? Are you managing what He gave you to the best of your abilities? You must also keep an ongoing assessment of your obstacles. How often do you write things down in your journal? How can you hit a target you cannot see? Have you written down your list of seven obstacles? It is very important that you take time to study the failures of others, so you do not repeat their mistakes. Recommit to the good counsel found in God's word and recognize the things that serve as distractions in your life. It is time to head back out there!

GET IN THE GAME

You were created to keep yourself in the right environment. Your environment has a tremendous impact on your mind. The environments you find yourself in are a choice, so choose wisely. What books are you reading? What type of entertainment are you spending your downtime on? What friendships and habits do you need to examine and possibly remove from your life? To stop means to give up or cease movement. Do not stop!

MINDSET: Get up early each day and be productive with your time. Hold yourself accountable. Stop comparing what you got to what they got. Meditate on God's word. Commit to overcoming one through six on your list, and once you have reached that point, keep going.

THE WORLD AND FATHERLESSNESS

"I believe in God not because my parents told me, not because the church told me, but because I've experienced His goodness and mercy for myself."

Unknown

This lesson is designed to encourage and lead you to open another book more frequently.

A FATHER IN THE TEXT

What does the Scripture say about the responsibilities of being a father? They are to set the example on living a good life. They are to be teachers and providers for the entire family. They are to instill discipline and work ethic in their children. One of the most profound descriptions I have found in the Bible is in 1 Chronicles 29. In the text, you find King David praying for his son, Solomon. Verse 19 says this, "Give my son Solomon the wholehearted desire to obey all your commands, laws, and decrees, and to do everything necessary to build this Temple, for which I have made preparations." Children who know their fathers pray for them consistently feel loved and secure. Unfortunately, in the reality of the world we live in, the image of a father is far from the outline of what a father should look like that we see in Scripture. So, how do we restore it?

YOUR WORLD

Do your research and know the facts. Educate your mind and pray for the desire to make a difference. The major two causes of fatherlessness in the last fifty years can be narrowed down to divorce and births out of wedlock. Fatherlessness can be described as the state of not having a father in the home. Did you know that children are four times more likely to live below the poverty line if the father is not around? How many single mothers do you know personally? The point of this is to open your mind to the reality of fatherlessness that exists all around you. 1 Timothy 5 gives us some great advice about widows and elders in our community. Many people think the Bible is outdated and not relevant to the world today – however, it is just as relevant and real as the latest Netflix show everyone is binge watching. Don't believe me? Then I want to encourage you to read more Scripture. Specifically, the topics in the Bible that shine a positive light on what it looks like to be a good father.

YOUR REPSONSE

Do you delight in the law of the Lord? I challenge you to read and write each of these verses seven times. Proverbs 23:24, Psalm 127:3-5, Joshua 24:15, Matthew

23:9, and John 3:16. There are so many more, but I truly believe these will give you a good start and a fresh perspective on the importance of fatherhood. Men were created to elevate others. Men were created to expect excellence. Men were created to love their life's work. Men were created to learn from the best. Men were created to be leaders in their communities. Men were created to read and write. We all have an amazing Heavenly Father who has given us life and opportunity!

MINDSET: Walk in this promise today. Psalm 2:7-8, "The king proclaims the Lord's decree. 'The Lord said to me, "You are my son. Today I have become your father. Only ask, and I will give you the nations as your inheritance, the whole earth as your possession."'"

WORDS OF WISDOM

"Act as if what you do makes a difference. IT DOES."

William James

Your daily actions determine a lot more than you think!

FIGHT FOR IT

What does it mean to be in a fight? It simply means to become involved in the exchange of physical blows or the use of weapons against an opponent. Whether you realize it or not, there is a fight you must start doing a much better job of maintaining, and it is not a physical one. Notice that it is more about mental maintenance than a fixed position. This means you must dedicate yourself to the renewing of your thoughts every single morning as soon as you wake up. Once you get into the routine of doing this in the morning time, strive to renew your mind before bed as well. 2 Timothy 1:7 says this: "For God has not given us a spirit of fear, but of power and of love and of a sound mind." Your mind is your greatest weapon and you must get involved in your community if you are going to make a difference in its future. Where you are located right now is not an accident. Figure out what you need to fight for this week and use your mind to focus on a strategy for success.

ALTITUDE

The word altitude means reaching a great height. Remind yourself of this truth as often as possible: you were not created to live a mediocre, boring, and under-achieving life. You were created to soar to great heights and your actions are intimately connected to your influence. The Wright brothers are well known for their innovative influence on the field of aviation. In 1903, they successfully flew the first airplane. Neither Wilbur nor Orville Wright attended college. My point is this: you do not need to have more degrees than a thermometer to influence the world around you. You can make a difference with the gifts God gave you. However, if you fall into the attitude of comparison, you will tend to fly lower than you are capable of on a consistent basis. You need to have the attitude of a champion. Champions are always prepared for turbulence and they handle themselves like a skilled pilot.

AWARENESS

You are the pilot of your mind, and once you become aware of this, you will begin to take flight. You will never make a difference in this world without daily actions. When you are gone, how do you want the people who love you the most to remember you? The point of awareness is that it is an ongoing process; a process that seeks to renew your mind with information you can use to influence those around you. Learning to stay calm in high-pressure situations is an invaluable gift. Your demeanor will impact your environment, for good or for bad. People who complain and shift the blame on others are not really cut out to make a positive difference in this world. In conclusion, we cannot always control the events in our lives, but we can control our response to every event. Attitude determines altitude!

MINDSET: The outcome you want lies within your ability to respond in a positive manner. Your actions matter!

NO OPPORTUNITES WASTED

"Trying hard and working hard is its own reward. It feeds the soul. It affirms your will and your power. And it radiates from you, lighting the way for all those who see you."

Charles M. Blow

If you knew today was your last day on earth, how would you act and what legacy would you leave?

LEGACY 101

A legacy is essentially the story of someone's life. A descriptive list of the many things that person did right, as well as the things they did wrong. These are the very details that are left behind and how a person will be remembered. Leave your mark. Leave your mark. Leave your mark. Teach with your life and let the good outweigh the bad. The pen is literally in your hands!

GOOD NEWS REMINDER

God loves you, you were created in His image, and you can achieve anything you want to if you have faith. Let us examine the following three words as we renew our mentality headed into this week. Believing, burdens, and boldness. **Believing** means a state of mind in which trust or confidence is placed in some person or thing. **Burdens** means to carry something heavy or deal with something difficult. **Boldness** means to not be afraid of difficult situations. What is the hardest thing you are going through right now? Take time to intentionally think about it. Why? Because it is critical to be aware of the burdens in your life. The burdens we carry often lead us directly to our purpose in life. In Matthew 11:28, Jesus said: "Come to me, all of you who are weary and carry heavy burdens, and I will give you rest." You can boldly have confidence that Christ is within you and you are enough!

LISTEN CAREFULLY

The promise God spoke over your life still stands. No bad day, no unfortunate news, no mistakes you have made, and no burden you are carrying can stop you from receiving His promises. In Hebrews 4:1 it says: "God's promise of entering His rest still stands." This week especially, I encourage you to not waste any opportunities to focus on your promise. Your promise is always available, but you must intentionally train your mind to focus on it. What is your reason to smile? You need to focus on your reason. A purpose that is far greater than your pain. It is time for you to continue walking in a manner worthy of your calling. Unknowingly, you will begin to shine your light for others to see. They need your example. Let your life bring good news into the lives of those around you. Leave your mark and make it a positive one that will be hard to forget!

MINDSET: People will not remember every detail of your life. They will surely forget some of the things you said and did. However, they will never forget how you made them feel. Make them feel like they matter. Make them feel loved. Take every opportunity to pour into someone else. The more of yourself you give to others, the more this life will give back to you. Your reward will be great!

GET READY, GET READY, GET READY

"I will prepare and someday my chance will come."

Abraham Lincoln

Disciplined thinking is the key to becoming the best version of yourself. If you will consistently train your mind to think positively, you will see faster results. You cannot hit a home run if you will not swing at the ball. What leadership opportunities are you hoping for? Will you be prepared if you are given that chance today?

SEE YOURSELF THERE

You must learn to visualize yourself in the places you want to be. Visualization can be defined as the formation of a mental image of something. Start seeing yourself as an overcomer of difficult obstacles. Start seeing yourself as a good husband or wife. Start seeing yourself happy with your life's work. Start seeing yourself as a champion. Once you begin to visualize where you want to go, you must pause and make sure your priorities are in line with your desired destination. If they are not in line, then things tend to take much longer to happen.

PRIORITY AND PREPARATION

To prioritize something means to regard one thing as more important than the other. When we look at the life of Jesus Christ in the Scriptures, it is evident He prioritized prayer. So, what exactly is prayer and how does it apply to our lives today? Write this down: prayer is learned, and Jesus gave us an outline. The disciples were given a specific pattern of prayer procedures in what we know as the Lord's prayer. It is true that prayer can and should be done in a group setting; however, we have been taught a greater lesson about what to do as individuals. In Matthew 6:6 it says: "But when you pray, go away by yourself, shut the door behind you, and pray to your Father in private. Then your Father, who sees everything, will reward you." Prioritize an hour or more each day to prayer and quiet time. This time will prepare you for what lies ahead in your life. Before you go any further this week, take a moment to allow God's word to pinpoint your priorities and adjust as needed.

PROXIMITY

When you pray properly and prioritize properly, it is like making an unstoppable investment. Like a seed that goes into the ground, eventually it will come up and become something other than a seed. The word proximity simply means closeness. Listen clearly to what I am about to say next: you are closer than you think you are. Why do you think Jesus told us to pray like this: "on earth as it is in heaven"? Because we are to build great things in our lives with the time we are given. God needs access to your body, heart, mind, and spirit. Do you have a secret quiet place that you go to consistently to access His presence? Do you keep a weekly journal? Do you take the time to renew your mind in the morning and at night? Find your place, shut the door, and go to work. Hebrews 4:12 says this: "For the word of God is alive and powerful. It is sharper than the sharpest two-edged sword, cutting between soul and spirit, between joint and marrow. It exposes our innermost thoughts and desires." Once we get ourselves in agreement with God, He will give us a return on our investment.

IT IS TIME

God loves you so much that He has given you this day. He wants you to be intentional about every thought you allow to enter your mind. If you will commit to keeping your mind in a positive place, He will position you for greatness. The ups and downs you have experienced in your life are simply preparation for what is about to happen next. Stay disciplined internally; only thinking about things that are honorable and pure. Keep practicing the art of readiness, and it will pay off!

MINDSET: Work hard and serve others today in enthusiasm. Your time to shine is coming!

WHY WE EXIST

"The world that Christ died for was a
world that is multi-colored."

Dr. Rice Brooks

Do a quick examination of your family, your closest
friends, and the other people you frequently asso-
ciate with. Do you think it is a diverse group of individuals? How do you think you can diversify it even more?
We must all be intentional about prioritizing diversity
in our everyday lives.

DIVERSITY

Diversity is simply defined as a variety of different
things. God's creation is very diverse, consisting of a
multitude of ethnicities, languages, cultures, talents,
etc. I want to encourage you to begin valuing diversity
in as many areas of your life as possible. Your friendships should display diversity in occupations, upbring-
ings, and mentalities. You must learn how to surround
yourself with people who do not think like you. This

is a learned skill set that is only developed over time. Today, people tend to become divided about the silliest things. For example, what school your kids go to, what sports you prefer over another, what foods people should eat, disagreements about religious beliefs, differences in political views, etc. One major issue that has plagued our communities globally for far too long is the issue of racial inequality and injustice. Did you know that race is not actually a biblical term? This term came from Charles Darwin in the 1800s. My point is this: always consider the source of your information. When Jesus walked the earth, there was no greater divide than between the Jews and Gentiles. This ongoing issue has been around for too long. I believe the Bible has the answer!

HOW DO I FIX IT?

We cannot fix the issues of mankind by ourselves. However, we can learn to become vessels of change within a greater unified community. Around the time Jesus called the first disciples into action, there was great distrust between the Jews and Gentiles. Many Jewish people thought of the Gentiles as unclean and unworthy people. Today, the label of Jew and Gentile may not be relevant to you, but the culture of division still exists. Galatians 3 gives us clear instructions on how we should respond to division of any kind. Verse 28 is profound: "In Christ's family there can be no division into Jew and non-Jew, slave and free, male and female. Among us you are all equal. That is, we are all in a common relationship with Christ." Are you still thinking about how you can become part of the change and broaden your sphere of influence? The answer is simple and complex at the same time – live for Christ. Do you realize you are an ambassador for Christ? An ambassador is an accredited person sent by a country as their official representative.

ON EARTH AS IT IS

Build the Kingdom right where you are. Where some see a relationship that is unsalvageable, you can see opportunity for reconciliation. Where others see failure, you can see a chance to beat Goliath. Where the world sees a person's shortcomings, you can see the best part of them. Where the world walks by sight, you can shine your light for others to see. Today, I want to challenge you to read and reflect upon the Lord's Prayer. Remember: we are all one creation and diversity is a good thing. Do not think about heaven as some far away destination you will arrive at once you leave this place. Instead, think about the possibility of creating God's Kingdom in your current community context. The people in your life are what is most important. Today, you have an opportunity to be a vessel for God's glory and to touch someone's heart.

TOUCH THE WORLD

Be available to others. Being available for someone is to willingly give them your time. Time is the most precious resource we have on this earth, and we must all use it wisely. Jesus provided us with a perfect example of how to serve others' needs above our own. We have all been given the mandate of reconciliation. So, use your life and your abilities to connect the dots for those around you. Love people by being a good listener and look for ways to encourage them daily. This is our purpose on earth: to be there for each other. Remember this: everyday matters!

MINDSET: If you want to get a glimpse of your future, take a closer look at your friendships. You will have a greater impact on the world if you diversify your team with the right people. Choose wisely!

THE ENVIRONMENT MATTERS

> "God grant me the serenity to accept the
> things I cannot change, the courage to
> change the things I can, and the wisdom
> to know the difference."

Napoleon Hill

o not worry about _____.

QUIT LOSING SLEEP

How do you fill in the blank? Your answer may be
different from mine and those around you; however,
there is a better way to live. Start developing a wor-
ry-free mindset. Worrying is an ongoing dialogue in
your mind that can be corrected if you are willing to
train yourself through study and meditation. When you
begin to intentionally focus your eyes on what is positive in your life, your body will be filled with light. Your
mind needs light to function. Each morning, you need
to wake up early and maximize the day. If you spend
the first thirty minutes each morning scrolling social

media and the news, it will have a negative impact on your mind. If you find yourself up late at night struggling to sleep, I want to encourage you to replace how you start your day.

FIX YOUR THOUGHTS

Philippians 4:8 says this: "And now, dear brothers and sisters, one final thing. Fix your thoughts on what is true, and honorable, and right, and pure, and lovely, and admirable. Think about things that are excellent and worthy of praise." Replacing worry with confidence and hope is the better way to live. Here are some practical ways to think differently. Count your blessings in the morning. Focus on doing and giving more than you get paid for at your job. Laugh at yourself. Look intentionally for the good in everyday adversity. Never clutter your mind with uncontrollable soil. Fill it with good thoughts!

TILL THE SOIL OF YOUR MIND

To till the land is to cultivate the conditions of the ground and produce crops. Similarly, your mind works like the earth beneath you, as it can be highly productive. Your environment can be described as the set of circumstances and conditions by which you are surrounded. Anyone can rent a light duty tiller from a home improvement store for about $60 per day. However, tools like this typically require a deposit of $150 up front. The company will keep this money if you damage their property. My point is this: you will always pay more in the long run for not managing your thoughts appropriately. Your mind is like a garden and you must regularly maintain the soil. If not, you risk the dirt becoming too hard for seeds to grow abundantly. We cannot always control what is going on around us, but we can learn how to respond in a positive manner. Go to the book of Luke and find chapter 8. Take ten minutes to read the parable of the farmers scattering seed. If you patiently accept this word as true, it will produce great understanding within you. Ultimately, you are only going to be as successful as you think in your mind!

MINDSET: As you think in your mind, so you will be!

GROW WHERE YOU ARE PLANTED

"What you get by achieving your goals is
not as important as what you become by
achieving your goals."

Zig Ziglar

You can either go through the week or you can
grow through the week. Are you going, or are
you growing?

SCATTER

To scatter something means to throw it in various
random directions. As you strive to reach your short-
term and long-term goals, you must learn how to
become planted. To plant something means to place it
within the ground so that it can grow. The term *growth*
indicates a lengthy process. Your mind cannot be scattered, disorganized, or distracted. You must focus!

FIXED POSITION

We live and work where we do for a purpose that is far greater than we can ever imagine. The problem many of us run into in our process of becoming great in our endeavors is the issue of impatience. We live in a microwave society that tries to trick us into believing success will come to us easily. This is a cultural mindset that must be corrected within our communities. Just because our dreams are still in seed form does not mean they will not grow into great trees over time. One of the largest trees in the entire world is the General Sherman sequoia tree. It can be found in California's Sequoia National Park, standing almost 300 feet tall. In mathematics, the term *volume* can be defined as a three-dimensional space enclosed by a boundary or occupied by an object. The volume of the German Sherman is about half the volume of an Olympic-sized swimming pool. It is estimated that this tree has been around for over 2,000 years. So, why are we in such a hurry?

LET THE DIRT WORK

Life is challenging, difficult, tiresome, and downright ugly sometimes. Are we willing to get dirty? For most of us, we must realize that any seed we plant will require more time than we would like. Patience is hard, but it is a necessary requirement for every great accomplishment. In Matthew 13, Jesus sat beside a lake and started teaching. The Scriptures say that so many people started to gather around Him, He got into a boat and began to teach from the shoreline. As those people drew closer, He began to tell them about the parable of a farmer scattering seed. Verse 4 says: "As he scattered them across his field, some seeds fell on a footpath, and the birds came up and ate them." Verse 7 says: "Other seeds feel among thorns that grew up and choked out the tender plants." My point is this: when our seed finds the right soil, it will produce a mind-blowing amount of results. However, it is not what we get in life, but what we become in the process of all our getting.

MINDSET: God wants to bless you 100 times more than you would believe based on your own human logic. Read Isaiah 55:8 and then pray for patience to remain where you are currently planted. You must continue to scatter your seed, but never allow your mind to become scattered. Reorganize your thoughts and trust God!

HEART, SOUL, STRENGTH, MIND

"And he answered, "You shall love the Lord your God with all your heart and with all your soul and with all your strength and with all your mind, and your neighbor as yourself."

Luke 10:27

Family is the foundation of your strength.

HEART AND SOUL

Your heart is an essential component for sustaining your life. Keeping your heart in a healthy state is something you can work on every day. The things you eat and how often you move have a great impact on your longevity. Family is the heart and soul of a community. Do you know how to incorporate your soul in all your weekly actions? Take a deeper look at how you can accomplish that. The letter **S** in *soul* stands for *selfless*. To be selfless is to be more concerned with the needs and wishes of others than your own. The letter **O** in *soul* stands for *opportunity*. Look for opportunities this week to show love to everyone in your life. Handwrite someone a letter of encouragement. Send your spouse a gift at work. Pay for someone's coffee. Find a way to bring joy into the conversation. The letter **U** stands for *united*. There is a powerful wave of unstoppable energy when people are connected to accomplish a common goal. Be unified in all your endeavors. Finally, the letter **L** stands for *leadership*. Leadership can be described as the process of using your influence to maximize the efforts of others to reach a set list of goals. Treat everyone you come across this week like they are an important part of your family; especially those who do not think like you.

STRENGTH OF MIND

Start to develop a champions mindset. Champions learn how to see failure as steppingstones to success. Champions learn to envision prosperity during seasons of turmoil and pain. Envision the problems in your life as a part of God's plan. Monitor your progress, remain humble, and expect a payoff. Part of loving the people you lead involves making tough decisions that impact many different people in a variety of ways. Along the journey, you will only learn through the willingness to make honest mistakes. Eventually, you will learn to avoid repeats, if you stay true to your core beliefs and convictions. Who do you call family? What cracks do you have in your family foundation that need repairing? What practical steps can you take to be selfless this week? Are you willing to become weak so someone else can become strong? Treat the people in your life with honor, respect, and most importantly, with love.

MINDSET: We will ultimately be measured by the positive impact we have on each other and the community. Loving hard is the secret to all success!

LIVING GENEROUSLY

"Don't just aspire to make a living, aspire
to make a difference."

Denzel Washington

Have you read any of Dave Ramsey's financial resources? He is a multi-millionaire with an immense amount of sound advice on the topic of finances.

LEARN TO MANAGE IT

You are a steward of what you are given. Another word for steward is manager. Stewardship is the task of supervising or taking care of something important. One example of stewardship is managing the staff of a large estate. One of Ramsey's best quotes about money: "you will either learn to manage money, or the lack of it will manage you." Do you agree or disagree? Why?

THE FIRST TEN

The first ten minutes of your day set the tone for the rest of the day. The thoughts that you have when you immediately wake up are critical to your success each week. We should all go to bed thankful for what we already have, but we should also dream about the good things to come. Many of us have elaborate dreams, but most of us do not have the proper work ethic required to make them a reality. Did you know that Jesus talked about money in eleven of the thirty-nine parables? If you are going to start to live more generously, you are going to have to fully understand the principle of the first fruits. In the Old Testament, in the book of Malachi, chapter 3 gives us sound advice on how we are to manage all our possessions – which includes our money. The word *tithe* simply means one tenth. Giving the first portion of your income is the starting point for financial prosperity. If God can get it through you, He will get it to you. I pray that you will take ten minutes to allow this Scripture to speak to your heart, mind, and spirit before going any further this week. Apply the first ten rule to every area of your life and watch God exceed your expectations.

YOU CAN BE GENEROUS

What do you treasure? Some treasure job titles, others treasure worldly recognition. We all treasure something, whether we realize it or not. Being generous is to show kindness towards others. It is living in a state of readiness to give more of something, such as money or time, than is logically expected. Jesus told us our hearts are storage containers for the things we most dearly treasure. In Luke 6, Jesus teaches us that whatever we give will be given back to us. If we give our time, we will get time. If we give hate, we will get hate in return. If we give money, we will get more money. The point is that we must be intentional about what we give and why we give it. Take a few moments to write down a list of things you currently oversee. Some examples to help you think: your salary, your household, your employees, your business, etc. Now take a moment to consider how well you are managing those things. Now, commit to being a better manager!

MINDSET: *Being blessed is not a bad thing. God wants you to prosper. However, in all your getting, be sure to get an understanding of how you can live generously.*

AT YOUR SERVICE

"Small acts, when multiplied by millions
of people, can transform the world."

Howard Zinn

Humility is not popular in today's culture. This week's lesson is designed to create awareness around your acts of service. The goal is to develop and prioritize humility in our daily lives. How can we accomplish this?

BE HUMBLE

It is easy for someone to say they are humble, but how can you see the evidence of it in their lives? Humility is all about the posture of your mind. Posture is people's way of doing things and the attitude they express while in the action of completing them. To be humble is to place yourself in a lower position and willingly serve the requests of others. A servant is an individual who willingly works to complete various tasks given by others. Here are some practical ways you can see evidence of humility in the lives of others: spends time listening to others, always available to help, makes every effort to show thankfulness, accepting of feedback, and operating with an abundance mentality.

BE THE CHANGE

In Matthew 23, Jesus criticized the religious leaders of that day. He highlighted how they knew the law but did not follow it with their life's example. He told the crowds and His disciples to not follow their examples. He went on to expose how they did everything for show, and this is exactly what we need to address before we move any further. To create positive change in the world, we must not serve others and immediately expect to be recognized for it. Being recognized is nice, but it is not what Jesus had in mind when teaching us about the importance of our acts of service. Matthew 23:11 says: "The greatest among you must be your servant." There is a question we must constantly ask ourselves: *Who are we supposed to be serving and how should we do it?*

BE AN AGENT OF TRANSFORMATION

God's word has the power to renew your mind. You were created to serve others with all your energy, fortitude, and strength. Your mind will be transformed through your willing obedience to serve your community. If you follow these three steps, I am confident God will clearly show you how to respond. Step 1: Be faithful over the small things in life. Step 2: Willingly make yourself available to others. Step 3: Operate with an abundance mentality. It is possible to be a good servant and feel like you are in the land of just enough.

Your immediate needs may be supplied, and you seem to be doing better than most folks. However, in the back of your mind you are still hoping for much more. Stay faithful, do not give up, and keep doing the little things, day in and day out. Your daily presence represents a positive change in your community. You are capable of dramatically changing the character of our culture. Your willingness to consistently remain humble has an impact that stretches farther than your eyes can see. Live today as if it were your last!

MINDSET: Seek opportunities and create change in our culture. The next generation is counting on you!

WEEK 42

LEAVE IT BEHIND

"Failure is part of the process. You just learn to pick yourself up. And the quicker and more resilient you become, the better you are."

Michelle Obama

Move forward with a fresh way of thinking. You cannot move in a forward direction if you are too busy focusing on what is behind you. Did you know that a well-handled failure is your connecting point to triumphant success?

A WORSHIPPER

What we initially discern as positive sometimes turns out to have many negative impacts on our lives. Conversely, what we initially discern as negative often turns out to be some of the best things that ever happen in our lives. My point is this: do not judge a circumstance by its cover. To discern is to perceive or recognize something. You are not going to be able to control everything that occurs in your environment. Each environment you find yourself in most frequently will come with its own set of challenges. My challenge to you is to learn how to worship while you wait. Whether we recognize it or not, we all worship something. Honor God with your worship and the way you think.

A WARRIOR

What voices in your life are telling you that you do not have a chance in the fight you are currently in? Hear what I am about to say: without a conflict, you will never become a conqueror. Extraordinary conflict has the ability to produce extraordinary character. For David, it was Saul telling him he was ridiculous for even trying to go out and fight Goliath. 1 Samuel 17:33 says: "Don't be ridiculous! Saul replied. There's no way you can fight this Philistine and possibly win! You're only a boy, and he's been a man of war since his youth." It is not the big moments that help us become resilient. It is the little moments where no one is watching us that ultimately guide us through difficult times. You must learn how to use your mind to help you recover quickly from difficult criticisms. See, David knew he was ready for the fight, because he had been killing lions and bears while protecting his father's livestock for years before that day. David recognized he was not made in that moment, but in the years, months, and weeks that came before it.

A WINNER

When is the last time you tried something that was bound to fail without divine intervention? Even when the odds are stacked against you, God can use a winning mentality to defy those odds. 1 Samuel 17:50 says: "When the Philistines saw their champion was dead, they turned and ran." David had a way of thinking that was much different than Saul's. Saul thought if he could not defeat Goliath, then surely little David could not. Winning is a way of thinking, and what you were put here to do. Winning is all about courage and resilience in the face of great difficulties. Do not be limited by the thinking of others. People will often discount you because they have discouraged themselves. Stop looking for your power to come from the outside, and start looking for His power to flow from within you.

MINDSET: You are here because of the little moments.

THE EDGE OF THE BLESSING

"Stop letting negative people that don't believe in themselves talk you out of believing in you."

Keion Henderson

Take your thoughts back today and stop allowing negative people to impede your progress.

FOCUS AND FAITH

You must learn how to use your mind to operate like a light switch. History was made in 1884 when John Henry Holmes invented the first light switch using quick break technology. Electricity is the presence and flow of an electric charge. Electricity is capable of transferring energy from one thing to another. Your faith can serve as a light to your community. Literally, any place you go, you have the power within you to make it better. However, you will only make them better if you learn how to focus your mind and flip the switch when a negative thought comes. What battles are you currently fighting? What difficulties stand in the way of your next goal? What is really stopping you from the blessings you hope and pray for each week? Write this down and put it on your bathroom mirror. *The only thing that can stop you from God's blessings in your life is you.*

CAN'T LOSE MENTALITY

Take your thoughts back. It is critical to understand the origin of every negative thought that enters your conscious mind. Your conscious mind holds all the feelings, memories, and thoughts you are currently aware of. Essentially, it contains everything within your awareness. Focus on that awareness and learn how to flip the switch. Be a conduit for strong moral character and good things will happen for you.

MINDSET: You must learn to manage where you are before you ask God to take you where you want to go!

THE POWER OF LEANING

"Trust in the Lord with all your heart and lean not on your own understanding; in all your ways acknowledge him, and he will make your paths straight."

Proverbs 3:5

The direction in which you lean will determine where you end up. To lean is to incline or bend from a vertical position. Are you mindful of the amount of time you spend on both your vertical and horizontal relationships?

WHEN YOU ARE NOT STRONG

Although we have a multitude of responsibilities, we cannot take care of anyone else if we do not first take care of ourselves. Even as we make a conscious effort to maintain self-care, there will be days when we are mentally, physically, and spiritually exhausted. For those types of days, we must learn how to properly recharge our minds. Eating a variety of nutritious meals, living an active lifestyle, and maintaining a healthy sleeping schedule will help us recharge physically. However, how do we go about recharging our minds and spirits? There is a buried treasure in the earth found within the pages of the Bible. One of my favorite treasures is found in Matthew 13:44. Jesus spoke these eye-opening words: "The kingdom of heaven is like treasure hidden in a field. When a man found it, he hid it again, and then in is joy went and sold all he had and bought the field." As men, and women, we will always be children to the God of the universe. I truly believe He wants us to diligently seek out our field and build our lives upon it. There is a king and queen within every one of us, but life is a process in which we are either growing stronger or wearier.

MY WEAKNESS AND HIS POWER

What may appear as your one insurmountable weakness is a perfect canvas for God's strength. A canvas is a strong cloth used to create a surface for oil painting. Just like a car needs oil and gas to operate, your mind needs the oil that comes from the things you choose to lean upon. Are you leaning on the news? Are you leaning on word of mouth and gossip? Are you leaning on God's word? Whether we recognize it or not, we are all leaning on something, so lean on things that are eternally true and never changing. You do not need to be perfect or have it all figured out. As a matter of fact, if we had every answer, we would not need God. I challenge you to lean harder than you have ever leaned in your life, but do not lean on your comprehension of your current set of circumstances. Instead, lean into the buried treasure of God's word and find new strength!

MINDSET: As you walk the pathways of your life, you will have tough days. Days where you naturally become more aware of your weaknesses than the strength of your Creator. You must quickly correct that mindset and acknowledge it will all work out in due time. When you are not strong, God is, and He loves you dearly!

GUIDANCE AND GRACE

"Your word is a lamp to my feet and a
light for my path."

Psalm 119:105

You will need a well-thought-out strategy to obtain your greatest goals in life. However, guidance and grace are more important than your original plan.

WELCOME IT

Run your race, but do not hesitate to welcome God's guidance and grace with open arms. It is critical that we routinely feed our minds with positive words. Words are the most powerful things we possess as humans. The more positive words our minds take in, the more positive words we will ultimately put out. Psalm 143:8 says this: "Let the morning bring me word of your unfailing love, for I have put my trust in you. Show me the way I should go, for to you I entrust my life." If God's word created everything we see in the world, then why not welcome it with joy each morning before we begin the day? His word is so powerful and can be compared to the blade of a sharp sword. His word will keep your mind sharp!

TAKE YOUR SOUL VITAMINS

Soul vitamins = God's word. When you focus your eyes on God's word, it creates a protective layer around your heart. To stay away from gossip and negative talk, you must prioritize your inner circle. Get around people who encourage you to read Scriptures. Get around people who celebrate you. When you do these things, God will begin to guide you through every season in your life. There will be rough days and amazing days. When you have enough soul vitamins in your mind, you will always function at a higher level. You will be able to go into a bad situation with a positive mindset. You will be able to handle success with a humble spirit.

A SUBTLE REMINDER

The word *grace* means to receive unmerited and undeserved favor from God. Grace is a wonderful thing. Just in case you have forgotten, or you simply need to be reminded: you are a child of God who is wonderfully made, and His grace exists in your life. There is a great plan and purpose for your life that only manifests itself when you allow God to guide you. God has always been your biggest fan and you play for His team. Think of yourself as an important role player on God's franchise. Continue to be strong. Continue to live courageously. Remember that you are loved unconditionally. Be the leader your family needs. Leadership is not about perfection; it is about making the people around you better.

Let's get better today and continue pressing toward our goals. You were created to be a big success!

MINDSET: With the word lighting my path, I will surely be successful.

WEEK 46

LIVE TO IMPACT

"All evangelism is, is enjoying God around others who do not know him yet."

Kore Bendix

Aspire to impact others and enjoy the life you have been given. Did you know the devil is not afraid of how many Scriptures we can remember? He is only afraid of how many we will put into practice!

ENJOY YOUR LIFE

You were created to be happy. In all honesty, the bad days make the good days sweeter. Impact means to come into forcible contact with another object. As a human, you have the ability within you to have a strong effect on other people. As you enjoy your life, how will you influence the team of people around you? It would not be a good thing for you to use enjoyment as a platform for selfishness. It would be a good thing for you to train your mind to enjoy serving others' needs above your own. I want to encourage you to think of practical ways to elevate others. All competitive runners lift weights and practice specific distances before they enter a race. It is not that they simply train, but to what standard they hold themselves while doing those things. Just as a runner aims to train at a high level, you must teach yourself to practice God's commands in your daily walk of life.

RUN TODAY

One definition for evangelism is spreading the Christian gospel by public preaching. Another is to show the love of Christ in your daily actions. The point is this: How we act shows people a lot about where our joy comes from. What are you showing people as you run your race of life? This week, you have an opportunity to evangelize the people who are spectators at your race. Today, imagine yourself as an Olympic runner about to perform in a sold-out stadium. A stadium is a place where athletes go to compete at the highest level. God loves you so much He created a lane for you in this world that no one else can run in. Did you know you cannot run your race in somebody else's lane?

YOUR STADIUM

1 Corinthians 9:24-25 MSG says this: "You've all been to the stadium and seen the athletes race. Everyone runs; one wins. Run to win. All good athletes train hard. They do it for a gold medal that tarnishes and fades. You're after one that's gold eternally." As you move toward greater, accept every divine idea that comes into your mind. Allow those ideas to become planted in the fertile soil of righteous thinking. Find a

group of runners who have a similar pace as you. Find the time each day to focus on your driving force.

D.R.I.V.E.

Keep this acronym fresh on your mind this week. **Do** unto others as you would have them do to you. **Realize** that your race must be run by you and no one else. **Invest** an adequate amount of time in the training process. **Visualize** the finish line. **Exercise** your faith muscles.

MINDSET: Show up to your stadium and run to win!

THE PRESTIGE OF PROFESSIONALISM

"Professional is not a label you give yourself; it is a description you hope others
will apply to you."

David Maister

How often do you think you should be recognized
for all your hard work? Are you being faithful in
your field?

YOUR PRESTIGE

Someone's prestige can be described as their repu-
tation that arises from personal accomplishments, successes, and other favorable qualities. Everyone wants
to have a perfect record and never lose, but that is an
unrealistic way of thinking. My challenge to you this
week is to develop joy in your seasons of low recognition. Take a closer look at the professionalism of David
before he was a king. In the book of 2 Samuel, David
eventually became king, but this was many years after
Saul was king. Despite Saul's military successes, he was

disobedient and did not completely follow all the Lord's commands. Saul was thirty years old when he first became king, and his reign lasted for over forty years. The burning question now becomes: what was David doing so well to be recognized by God during that time?

FEELING PASSED UP

Samuel was the prophet God spoke through during those days. The Lord told Samuel to go find a man named Jesse, and then He would reveal to him which of his sons would become the next king. 1 Samuel 16:2 says: "But Samuel asked, 'How can I do that? If Saul finds out about it, he will kill me.'" Samuel ended up following through with what he was told. When he found Jesse, he was reminded of the fact that God does not judge us by our outward appearance. Continuing with the story, Jesse began to present his sons to Samuel, one by one. Samuel told him each time that this was not the one. Jesse had presented his seven sons to the prophet, and none of them were chosen. 1 Samuel 16:11 says: "Then Samuel asked, 'Are these all the sons you have?' 'There is still the youngest,' Jesse replied. 'But he's out in the fields watching the sheep and goats.' 'Send for him at once,' Samuel said. 'We will not sit down to eat until he arrives.'"

YOUR TIME IS SET

As soon as David got to the house, he was anointed as king. David would go on to beat Goliath with a small stone and a sling shot. If we were given everything, we would not know how to work for anything. Like David, I believe you have a set time to be recognized at the highest level. In the meantime, be a professional. Not receiving recognition can be a painful thing to process internally. Especially when you are working as hard as you can and serving the Lord in the small things. Like David, they may call on each of your brothers before you, and you may be the last name brought up at the table. But trust me, there is a substantial advantage from learning how to be successful in the fields of your struggle. God will suddenly bless you in unexpected ways, so continue to be faithful over the small things!

MINDSET: Be a P.R.O. while you are not being recognized as a king. Be <u>Persistent</u>, <u>Resilient</u>, and <u>Opportunistic</u>. Your time is right around the corner!

THE CHARACTER OF CONTENTMENT

"Not that I was ever in need, for I have learned how to be content with whatever I have. I know how to live on almost nothing or with everything."

Philippians 4:11

Your conscious contentment will sustain your life in three practical ways: physical health, personal integrity, and strategic focus.

YOUR HEALTH

Physically, much of the country we live in is ailing right now. Did you know more heart attacks occur in this country on Monday mornings than any other day and time of the week? I believe people allow their minds to become overwhelmed with work-related things they cannot control. The side effect of a blocked mind is an unhealthy body. Here is one thing you can control: your level of physical activity. It is critical to exercise your mind, body, and spirit every single day. To optimize your health, you will need to consistently practice self-discipline. Discipline is the middle name of every healthy person I know. To get your mind thinking about practical ways to be disciplined when it comes to your health. Here are some examples: read a positive book, lift those weights, run a 5k while listening to a sermon, and walk your dog in the neighborhood. Doing these types of things will certainly reduce your stress level and minimize anxiety. Your body is essentially the vehicle of your character. Most people lose their discipline in their thirties; not you, you are just getting started!

INTEGRITY AND STRATEGIC FOCUS

Integrity matters, especially when no one else is watching. I want to encourage you to be the best you can be at your job this week. Take a moment and ask yourself: how many hours will I spend at work this week? If you are going to maintain strong integrity; you cannot allow yourself to spend those precious hours operating in mediocrity. Instead, hold yourself to the highest standard. Develop a clear vision for what you want to accomplish in the short-term and long-term future. Some characteristics of men and women of integrity include being gracious, being respectful, being responsible, being honest, and hardworking. As you walk in integrity, make sure you follow your plan of action for success. Focusing on your strategy will always give you a competitive advantage. Focus on the controllable things in your life. Are you a giver or a taker? Are you uplifting or draining? Are you a believer or a doubter? No matter what you are currently going through, your character is completely up to you. Believe that your best days are coming, be confident in your contentment, and never get discouraged by how impossible something may look. Read Matthew 23:11-12 and have a great week!

MINDSET: Contentment is simply a mindset of happiness and satisfaction. Allow your character to exude joyful contentment in everything you do this week.

YEAR OF GRINDING

"Can you honestly say the environments
you are in will yield the kind of harvest
you are expecting?"

Dr. Eric Thomas

What type of harvest are you expecting one year
from today? What if this were the moment that
could change your life forever? Over the next twelve
months, I want you to take intentional steps every single
day to grind as hard as possible. Your grind is your work
ethic and ability to do more than is required or asked.

YOUR CALENDAR

This is the year to outwork the competition, day
in and day out. One year from now, your reward will
ultimately match the position of your thoughts. In
team sports, the goal is to always outwork other athletes and their respective programs. The greatest teams
must collectively possess the mindset of accountability.
They must elevate their thoughts and learn to enjoy the

training process if they are going to be crowned a champion at the end of the season. Using weightlifting as an example, the correct position is critical on every rep. Lifting a heavy weight off the ground requires getting low and using the leg and back muscles in a safe manner. One injury to a star player, and they could miss weeks of training and preparation. Attention to details is essential in any weight room. It is the same with your mind: you must learn to control your thoughts if you want the results of a champion. Your environment is the key!

THE CITY

You must be accountable to the city God placed you in and the people He gave you. You can accomplish this by working as hard as you can to cultivate the dream you have in that specific location. Cultivation is the process of growing something to harvest it later. In farming, cultivation involves the process of producing crops for a profit. In your life, cultivation will require imagination and resilience. How many good seeds will you sow this week? In three months, how much work will you have completed? How will you overcome adversity if you are not intentional with your daily walk? Champions grind harder than others, but they do so in the right environment. This year, you must surround yourself with other grinders and submerge yourself in dirt.

DIRTY WORK

It takes nine months for a baby to fully develop and go through the birthing process. It takes anywhere from two to four months for corn to reach the point of harvest. In China, they commonly grow bamboo trees.

The seed of this particular tree remains in the ground for nearly five years without any emergence from the ground. That is five years of watering with no results. An astonishing thing happens when it finally sprouts through the dirt. In six weeks' time it can grow more than seventy-five feet high with proper care. Here is my point: we must expect God to provide for us abundantly. Do you expect a great harvest in your life when it takes longer than you originally thought? Grind as hard as you can with the time you have in front of you. God's timing is not always logical, and our calendars can never predict abundant blessings. God created time so we would respect His ways!

MINDSET: God is not confined by your calendar, or time!

WEEK 50

FOCUS ON GOOD THINGS

"Good things are supposed to happen to me."

Les Brown

The power of one positive thought is immeasurable and can help regulate your mental focus. Did you know that life is not happening *to* you, it is happening *for* you? I want to encourage you to take five minutes to read Romans 8:18 and 8:28 before you go any further.

ALL TOGETHER

Unify your mind with the word of God and allow the divinely inspired words to breathe fresh thoughts into your spirit. How can God work all things together for your good? As a human, I cannot fully explain the adversities and complexities of life. However, I do know that every adverse situation helps foster growth in our minds. When something negative happens, ask yourself the following questions: What can I learn from this experience? Is this situation even within my control?

How can I turn this set of circumstances into a positive outcome? What can I do to make a positive difference? Asking the right questions will allow you to develop a more positive mindset. When your faith is under pressure, your mindset is key. When your faith is under pressure, remind yourself that good things are supposed to happen to you. When your faith is under pressure, consider it as a gift from God. After all, it is the difficulties in life that teach us how to appreciate the good times.

THE RIGHT CULTURE

The community you live in has a culture, but culture is fluid and must be maintained every day. The spirit of togetherness expedites the number of good things that flow into our lives. Find a culture where the "we" is more important than the "me," and stay there for as long as you can. Your destiny is tied to the culture you cling to!

MINDSET: Focus your mind only on good things. What you choose to focus on is what will multiply in your life!

ELEVATE THE ATMOSPHERE

"Every man must decide whether he will
walk in the light of creative altruism or in
the darkness of destructive selfishness."

Dr. Martin Luther King Jr.

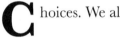**C**hoices. We all have them. Choose to be a light!

WHEN PEOPLE WALK AWAY

You have got to free your mind from the concept of
making everyone else happy. When negative and selfish
people walk away from your life, let them walk. Our
destinies are never attached to the people who walk
away. This does not necessarily mean they were bad
people. It simply means their role in your story has
come to an end. People will always disappoint you, and
that is exactly why we must decide to walk in the light
of God's word. In Matthew 5, Jesus sat down to talk to
His disciples. He gave them an image of being a light
in this world. Matthew 5:14 says: "You are the light of
the world. A city set on a hill cannot be hidden." You do

not need to hide what is in you any longer. It is time for you to choose to shine your light despite the darkness.

WHAT IS ALTRUISM ANYWAY?

This term, used by MLK, can be characterized as being concerned for the well-being of other people. Altruistic individuals put others' needs first and truly love the people around them. That is precisely the type of character we are called to display in our daily lives. In the beginning of Matthew 5, it talks about how Jesus went up on a mountain to get away from the crowds. God will always draw you to Himself and instruct you if you are willing to seek His will. Sometimes God does not bring us out of situations, but instead He brings us through them.

MINDSET: Once you have discovered the light within you, use it to illuminate the pathway for others.

WEEK 52

DEVELOPING DIRECTION

"I firmly believe you're never supposed to wish for more then you're willing to work for. Expectations should never exceed your effort."

Inky Johnson

One day you will look back and appreciate the process. The fact that you still have not quit should bring you joy!

FOR THE GLORY OF GOD

Sometimes we know where we would like to go but we have no idea how we will get there. If you seek God and remain grounded in His word, you will develop and maintain a strong sense of direction. Remember, what God has in store for you will not go to someone else. While you are working and waiting on your best days to come, make every effort to go above and beyond in the season you are currently in. Live for the glory of God alone and be content with the path He laid for you.

MAXIMUM EFFORT

Never share big dreams with small-minded people. They will typically try to talk you out of it or convince you that it will never happen. If you take one step, God will always take two. If you learn to overcome struggle, God will always bless you with success. Here is a short list of things that you may face this week: undeserved criticism, being misunderstood, being doubted, being lied on, etc. Overcome those obstacles with joy, make a maximum effort to honor God, and trust that He will keep you headed in the right direction.

TRUST FACTOR

The closer we get to our destination, the bumpier the road typically becomes. When you work hard and expect good things to happen, your dreams will begin to attract their own resources. Continue to trust God and keep going!

MINDSET: You will reach your destination because God will always guide you in the right direction.

Conclusion

EAGLES FLY ABOVE THE STORM

"God has already done everything He's going to do. The ball is now in your court. If you want success, if you want wisdom, if you want to be prosperous and healthy, you're going to have to do more than meditate and believe; you must boldly declare words of faith and victory over yourself and your family."

Joel Osteen

Thank you for purchasing this book. My hope is that this book would encourage you to open another book more often, the Bible. As you live your life, remember to slow down, and practice the discipline of renewing your mind.

MINDSET: It is time for you to fly high like an eagle!

References

Admin. "Kobe Bryant On Jersey Retirement: 'It's The One Thing You Can Control. You Are Responsible For How People Remember You-Or Don't. So Don't Take It Lightly." "." World Newj, August 26, 2020. https://www.worldnewj.com/kobe-bryant-on-jersey-retirement-its-the-one-thing-you-can-control-you-are-responsible-for-how-people-remember-you-or-dont-so-dont-take-it-lightly/.

Alepidis, Nikos. "17 Motivational Inky Johnson Quotes." Motivirus, March 6, 2020. https://motivirus.com/motivational-inky-johnson-quotes/.

Ambrose, Mark. "Community Resource Center, 218 Omohundro Pl, Nashville, TN (2020).", 218 Omohundro Pl, Nashville, TN (2020), 2017. https://www.govserv.org/US/Nashville/52740396441/Community-Resource-Center.

Augustine, Zachary G. "'You Have Power over Your Mind–Not Outside Events. Realize This and You Will Find Strength.'." Medium. Medium, March 24, 2017. https://medium.com/@zga/you-have-power-over-your-mind-not-outside-events-realize-this-and-you-will-find-strength-f17f75f03180.

Batterson, Mark. "Mark Batterson – Routines Are Normal, Natural, Healthy Th..." OffQuotes.com, August 31, 2019. https://offquotes.com/

mark-batterson-routines-are-normal-natu-ral-healthy-th/.

Bendix, Kore. "Evangelism." Brentwood: Tennessee, 2017.

Blow, Charles. "For Some Folks, Life Is a Hill." The New York Times. The New York Times, November 30, 2013. https://www.nytimes.com/2013/11/30/opinion/blow-for-some-folks-life-is-a-hill.html.

Broocks, Dr. Rice. *God's Not Dead: Evidence for God in an Age of Uncertainty*. Nashville, Tennessee: W Publishing Group, an imprint of Thomas Nelson, 2015.

Broocks, Rice, and Travis Thrasher. *Man, Myth, Messiah: Answering History's Greatest Question /CRice Broocks*. Nashville, TN, TN: W Publishing, an imprint of Thomas Nelson, 2016.

Church, Elevation. "Home." Steven Furtick Ministries, August 11, 2020. https://stevenfurtick.com/.

DUNGY, TONY. *ONE YEAR UNCOMMON LIFE DAILY CHALLENGE*. Place of publication not identified: TYNDALE MOMENTUM, 2019.

Em, David. "25 Motivational Eric Thomas Quotes." Next Level Gents, June 14, 2020. https://nextlevel-gents.com/eric-thomas-quotes/.

Flynn, Missy. "Why We Need To Rethink Our Ideas About 'Success' and 'Failure'." Grazia. Grazia, 2017. https://graziadaily.co.uk/life/real-life/can-learn-failure/.

Gardner, Steve. "Six Kobe Bryant Quotes That Define NBA Legend's Career." USA Today. Gannett Satellite Information Network, January 26, 2020. https://www.usatoday.com/story/sports/nba/2020/01/26/kobe-bryant-death-six-quotes-define-nba-legends-career/4582571002/.

Grace, Barbara. "Why 'Acting-as-If' Will Make You Twice As Successful." Medium. Medium, October 22, 2017. https://medium.com/@barbaragrace/are-you-acting-as-if-and-still-not-reaching-what-you-want-366e0347fa01.

Haden, Jeff. "Top 350 Inspiring Motivational Quotes to Tweet and Share." Inc.com. Inc., October 10, 2014. https://www.inc.com/jeff-haden/top-350-inspir-ing-motivational-quotes-to-tweet-and-share.html.

Henderson, Keion. *The Shift: Courageously Moving from Season to Season*. New York, NY: Worthy Publishing, 2020.

Jakes, T.D. "T. D. Jakes Quote." Lib Quotes, 2013. https://libquotes.com/t-d-jakes/quote/lbb4i7l.

Jakes, T.D. "TD Jakes–Cheering You On." Watch Christian Sermons Online (Sermons Archive), 2014. https://sermons.love/td-jakes/65-td-jakes-cheer-ing-you-on.html.

Jobs, Steve. "Steve Jobs." Wisdom Arts Leadership, July 1, 2014. https://www.wisdomartsleadership.com/words-of-wisdom/steve-jobs/.

Johnson, Amanda. "Small Acts." Outreach Outlet, 2012. http://outreachoutlet.ycdiapps.com/2018/07/18/

small-acts-when-multiplied-by-millions-of-people-can-transform-the-world-howard-zinn/.

Leung, Ally. "If You Take Responsibility for Yourself.–Les Brown." Lifehack. Lifehack, February 10, 2014. https://www.lifehack.org/articles/communication/you-take-responsibility-for-yourself-les-brown.html.

Lillis, Brock. "Unknown." Murfreesboro: Tennessee, n.d.

Mandela, Nelson. "6 Inspiring Quotes for Entrepreneurs from Nelson Mandela." Wamda, 2013. https://www.wamda.com/2013/12/6-inspiring-quotes-entrepreneurs-nelson-mandela.

Marston, Ralph. "Keep Going." The Daily Motivator, 1999. http://greatday.com/motivate/990109.html.

Martina, Antonio. "7 Eric Thomas' Quotes That Will Get You Through The Worst Of Times." Medium. Medium, January 22, 2020. https://medium.com/@antoniomartina/7-eric-thomas-quotes-that-will-get-you-through-the-worst-of-times-165858813d3d.

Maxwell, John. *Developing the Leader Within You*. Nashville, TN: HarperCollins Leadership, 2018.

McCarthy, Erin. "Roosevelt's 'The Man in the Arena.'" Mental Floss, April 23, 2015. https://www.mental-floss.com/article/63389/roosevelts-man-arena.

McLachlan, David. "Leadership Quote – Ken Blanchard on Servant Leadership." Lean CX, November 17, 2019. http://www.leancxscore.com/leadership-quote-ken-blanchard-on-servant-leadership/.

Meah, Asad. "50 Motivational Eric Thomas Quotes To Unleash Your Greatness." AwakenTheGreatnessWithin, August 4, 2016. https://www.awakenthegreatnesswithin. com/50-motivational-eric-thomas-quotes-to-unleash-your-greatness/.

Medrut, Flavia. "21 Vince Lombardi Quotes That Will Help You Achieve Excellence." Goalcast, November 1, 2019. https://www.goalcast.com/2018/05/30/ vince-lombardi-quotes-appreciate-excellence/.

Medrut, Flavia. "25 Abraham Lincoln Quotes to Make You Want to Be a Better Person." Goalcast, November 1, 2019. https://www.goalcast. com/2018/01/05/abraham-lincoln-quotes/.

Mercadante, Curt. "10 Quotes by Tom Rath That Will Inspire You to Find Your Strength." Medium. Medium, August 23, 2017. https://medium.com/@ curtmercadante/10-quotes-by-tom-rath-that-will-inspire-you-to-find-your-strength-381d1df72654.

Miller, written by Hunter. "Tim Allen Channels 'Home Improvement' Days in Latest Twitter Photo." Outsider, September 7, 2020. https://outsider.com/ news/tim-allen-channels-home-improvement-days-latest-twitter-photo/.

Mineo, Andy. "Lost." Atlanta: Georgia, n.d.

Osteen, Joel. "Ball In Your Court." Houston: Texas, n.d.

P, Johnny. "What You Get by Achieving Your Goals Is Not as Important." Personal Development Wisdom, December 1, 2016. https://

personaldevelopmentwisdom.com/achieving-your-goals-is-not-as-important.html.

Press, Word. "Character Cannot Be Developed in Ease and Quiet. Only through Experience of Trial and Suffering Can the Soul Be Strengthened, Ambition Inspired, and Success Achieved. -Helen Keller." Pacingoutcomes's Blog, January 7, 2010. https://pacingoutcomes.wordpress.com/2010/01/06/character-cannot-be-developed-in-ease-and-quiet-only-through-experience-of-trial-and-suffering-can-the-soul-be-strengthened-ambition-inspired-and--success-achieved-helen-keller/.

R, Rajesh. "Aspire To Make A Difference – Denzel Washington." talk, 2017. https://taalk.com/denzel-washington-aspire-to-make-a-differ-ence-best-motivational-speech-ever/.

Ramsey, Dave. "Managing Money." Brentwood: Tennessee, n.d.

S, Pangambam. "Les Brown: Stop Negative Thinking and Believe in Yourself (Full Transcript)." The Singju Post, April 16, 2020. https://singjupost.com/les-brown-stop-negative-thinking-believe-full-tran-script/?singlepage=1.

Saban, Nick. "Investing Time." Tuscaloosa: Alabama, n.d.

Saltos, Gabriela Landazuri. "MLK, Jr. Asked Us 'What Are You Doing For Others?' Here's How We Answered." HuffPost. HuffPost, December 7, 2017. https://www.huffpost.com/entry/mlk-day-serving-others_n_6489236.

Slaughter, Michael. *Momentum For Life*. Nashville, TN: Abingdon Press, 2005.

Styles, Leva. "Must Read Book: 'You've Got to Be Hungry' by Les Brown." Medium. Medium, April 4, 2020. https://medium.com/@LevaStyles/must-read-book-youve-got-to-be-hungry-by-les-brown-fc75388efc73.

Team, TheraNest. "6 Mental Health Quotes That Will Inspire Your Clients." TheraNest, January 15, 2020. https://theranest.com/blog/6-mental-health-quotes-that-will-inspire-your-clients/.

Themrrodge, PT. "Good Things Are Supposed to Happen to You! (2 Min Read)." Millionaire's Digest, August 14, 2017. https://millionairesdigest.wordpress.com/2017/08/15/good-things-are-supposed-to-happen-to-you-2-min-read/.

Thomas, Eric. "T.G.I.M." Detroit: Michigan, n.d.

Tyree, Elizabeth. "'Every Man Must Decide Whether He Will Walk in the Light of Creative Altruism or in the Darkness of...'" Medium. Medium, November 22, 2016. https://medium.com/@etyree1/every-man-must-decide-whether-he-will-walk-in-the-light-of-creative-altruism-or-in-the-darkness-of-b15edde0ebb2.

Vitamins, Startup. "Startupvitamins." Startup Vitamins, April 26, 2018. https://startupquotes.startupvitamins.com/post/173317052976/there-will-be-obstacles-there-will-be-doubters.

Washington, Denzel. "Denzel Washington: 'If You Don't Fail, You're Not Even Trying.'." Sean Croxton, April 24, 2017. https://seancroxton.com/quote-of-the-day/122/.

Weiss, Dr. Trae. Thompsons Station: Tennessee, 2017.

Yaeger, Don. "You Will Never Outperform Your Inner Circle: Why Kevin Durant Joined The Warriors." Forbes. Forbes Magazine, June 14, 2018. https://www.forbes.com/sites/donyaeger/2018/06/14/you-will-never-outperform-your-inner-circle-why-kevin-durant-joined-the-warriors/.

CPSIA information can be obtained
at www.ICGtesting.com
Printed in the USA
BVHW040144091220
595179BV00011BA/968